MAMMALS

PRIMATES

Apes, Monkeys, Marmosets, Lemurs ...

PAT MORRIS, AMY-JANE BEER

GROLIER

Tarsiers have extremely
long hind legs, as shown here
by the spectral or Celebes tarsier (1)
and the western tarsier (2).

Published 2003 by Grolier,
Danbury, CT 06816
A division of Scholastic Library Publishing

This edition published exclusively for the school
and library market

Planned and produced by
Andromeda Oxford Limited
11–13 The Vineyard,
Abingdon, Oxon OX14 3PX

www.andromeda.co.uk

Copyright © Andromeda Oxford Limited 2003

Project Director: Graham Bateman
Editors: Angela Davies, Penny Mathias
Art Editor and Designer: Steve McCurdy
Cartographic Editor: Tim Williams
Editorial Assistants: Marian Dreier, Rita Demetriou
Picture Manager: Claire Turner
Picture Researcher: Vickie Walters
Production: Clive Sparling
Researchers: Dr. Erica Bower, Rachael Brooks, Rachael Murton, Eleanor Thomas

Origination: Unifoto International, South Africa

Printed in China

Library of Congress Cataloging-in-Publication Data

Morris, Pat.
    Mammals / [Pat Morris, Amy-Jane Beer, Erica Bower].
        p. cm. -- (World of animals)
    Contents: v. 1. Small carnivores -- v. 2. Large carnivores -- v. 3. Sea mammals -- v. 4.
Primates -- v. 5. Large herbivores -- v. 6. Ruminant (horned) herbivores -- v. 7. Rodents
1 -- v. 8. Rodents 2 and lagomorphs -- v. 9. Insectivores and bats -- v. 10. Marsupials.
    ISBN 0-7172-5742-8 (set : alk. paper) -- ISBN 0-7172-5743-6 (v.1 : alk. paper) -- ISBN
0-7172-5744-4 (v.2 : alk. paper) -- ISBN 0-7172-5745-2 (v.3 : alk. paper) -- ISBN
0-7172-5746-0 (v.4 : alk. paper) -- ISBN 0-7172-5747-9 (v.5 : alk. paper) -- ISBN
0-7172-5748-7 (v.6 : alk. paper) -- ISBN 0-7172-5749-5 (v.7 : alk. paper) -- ISBN
0-7172-5750-9 (v.8 : alk. paper) -- ISBN 0-7172-5751-7 (v.9 : alk. paper) -- ISBN
0-7172-5752-5 (v.10 : alk. paper)
    1. Mammals--Juvenile literature. [1. Mammals.] I. Beer, Amy-Jane. II. Bower, Erica.
III. Title. IV. World of animals (Danbury, Conn.)

QL706.2 .M675 2003
599--dc21

2002073860   Set ISBN 0-7172-5742-8

About This Volume

The primates include lemurs, monkeys, apes, and ourselves. They are mostly highly intelligent animals, active during the day. The majority live in the tropics, and apart from humans, there are no primates in North America or Australia and only one in Europe. Primates usually form groups, often with complex social behavior involving special roles for different individuals. Most primates have only one or two young at a time, and females may produce fewer than five young in their whole life. That is balanced by a high degree of care for the offspring, leading to good survival prospects. Nevertheless, primates are unable to breed rapidly to make up for major losses in their populations. The largest species are a little bigger than the average human; the smallest are scarcely larger than a mouse.

Primates feed on a wide variety of foods, including leaves, fruit, insects, and flesh. Many are highly adaptable and occur in a variety of habitats, but some are extremely specialized. Certain species are quite numerous and may even become pests. However, the majority of primates are declining in numbers due to habitat loss, hunting for meat, and collecting for zoos and the pet trade. A higher proportion of primates are officially recognized as Endangered than any other major group of mammals.

Contents

The golden lion tamarin is one of the world's most threatened mammals.

Some small cercopithecines: mustached monkey (1); Allen's swamp monkey (2); and gray-cheeked mangabey (3).

How to Use This Set

World of Animals: Mammals is a 10-volume set that describes in detail mammals from all corners of the earth. Each volume brings together those animals that are most closely related and have similar lifestyles. So all the meat-eating groups (carnivores) are in Volumes 1 and 2, and all the seals, whales, and dolphins (sea mammals) are in Volume 3, and so on. To help you find volumes that interest you, look at pages 6 to 7 (Find the Animal). A brief introduction to each volume is also given on page 2 (About This Volume).

Article Styles

Articles are of three kinds. There are two types of introductory or review article: One introduces large animal groups like orders (such as whales and dolphins). Another introduces smaller groups like families (The Raccoon Family, for example). The articles review the full variety of animals to be found in different groups. The third type of article makes up most of each volume. It concentrates on describing individual animals typical of the group in great detail, such as the tiger. Each article starts with a fact-filled **data panel** to help you gather information at-a-glance. Used together, the three article styles enable you to become familiar with specific animals in the context of their evolutionary history and biological relationships.

Data panel presents basic statistics of each animal

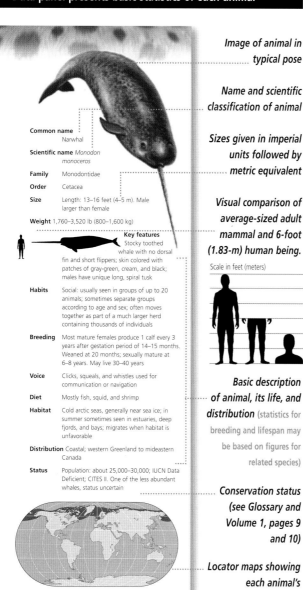

Image of animal in typical pose

Name and scientific classification of animal

Sizes given in imperial units followed by metric equivalent

Visual comparison of average-sized adult mammal and 6-foot (1.83-m) human being.

Basic description of animal, its life, and distribution (statistics for breeding and lifespan may be based on figures for related species)

Conservation status (see Glossary and Volume 1, pages 9 and 10)

Locator maps showing each animal's normal range

Common name Narwhal

Scientific name *Monodon monoceros*

Family Monodontidae

Order Cetacea

Size Length: 13–16 feet (4–5 m). Male larger than female

Weight 1,760–3,520 lb (800–1,600 kg)

Key features Stocky toothed whale with no dorsal fin and short flippers; skin colored with patches of gray-green, cream, and black; males have unique long, spiral tusk

Habits Social: usually seen in groups of up to 20 animals; sometimes separate groups according to age and sex; often moves together as part of a much larger herd containing thousands of individuals

Breeding Most mature females produce 1 calf every 3 years after gestation period of 14–15 months. Weaned at 20 months; sexually mature at 6–8 years. May live 30–40 years

Voice Clicks, squeals, and whistles used for communication or navigation

Diet Mostly fish, squid, and shrimp

Habitat Cold arctic seas, generally near sea ice; in summer sometimes seen in estuaries, deep fjords, and bays; migrates when habitat is unfavorable

Distribution Coastal; western Greenland to mideastern Canada

Status Population: about 25,000–30,000; IUCN Data Deficient; CITES II. One of the less abundant whales, status uncertain

Scale in feet (meters)

	6 (1.83)
	5 (1.5)
	4 (1.2)
	3 (0.9)
	2 (0.6)
	1 (0.3)

Article describes a particular animal

Scientific name of animal

Common name of animal

Captions to photographs provide additional information about each animal's lifestyle

Cross-references to relevant pages in this and other volumes

Easy-to-read and comprehensive text

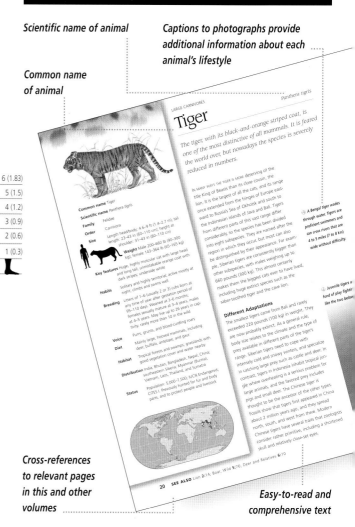

LARGE CARNIVORES

Panthera tigris

Tiger

The tiger, with its black-and-orange striped coat, is one of the most distinctive of all mammals. It is feared the world over, but nowadays the species is severely reduced in numbers.

IN MANY WAYS THE TIGER IS MORE deserving of the title King of Beasts than its close cousin, the lion. It is the largest of all the cats, and its range once extended from the fringes of Europe eastward to Russia's Sea of Okhotsk and south to the Indonesian islands of Java and Bali. Tigers from different parts of this vast range differ considerably, so the species has been divided into eight subspecies. They are named after the region in which they occur, but most can also be distinguished by their appearance. For example, Siberian tigers are consistently bigger than other subspecies, with males weighing up to 660 pounds (300 kg). This almost certainly makes them the biggest cats ever to have lived, including huge extinct species such as the saber-toothed tiger and the cave lion.

Different Adaptations

The smallest tigers came from Bali and rarely exceeded 220 pounds (100 kg) in weight. They are now probably extinct. As a general rule, body size relates to the climate and the type of prey available in different parts of the tiger's range. Siberian tigers need to cope with intensely cold and snowy winters, and specialize in catching large prey such as cattle and deer. In contrast, tigers in Indonesia inhabit tropical jungle where overheating is a serious problem for large animals, and the favored prey includes pigs and small deer. The Chinese tiger is thought to be the ancestor of the other types. Fossils show that tigers first appeared in China about 2 million years ago, and they spread north, south, and west from there. Modern Chinese tigers have several traits that zoologists consider rather primitive, including a shortened skull and relatively close-set eyes.

Common name Tiger

Scientific name *Panthera tigris*

Family Felidae

Order Carnivora

Size Length head/body: 4.6–9 ft (1.4–2.7 m); tail length: 23–43 in (60–110 cm); height at shoulder: 31–43 in (80–110 cm)

Weight Male 200–660 lb (90–300 kg); female 143–364 lb (65–165 kg)

Key features Huge, highly muscular cat with large head and long tail; unmistakable orange coat with dark stripes, underside white

Habits Solitary and highly territorial, active mostly at night; climbs and swims well

Breeding Litters of 1–6 (usually 2 or 3) cubs born at any time of year after gestation period of 95–110 days. Weaned at 3–6 months, males females sexually mature at 3–4 years, males at 4–5 years. May live up to 26 years in captivity, rarely more than 10 in the wild

Voice Purrs, grunts, and blood-curdling roars

Diet Mainly large, hooved mammals, including deer, buffalo, antelope, and gaur

Habitat Tropical forests and swamps; grasslands with good vegetation cover and water nearby

Distribution India, Bhutan, Bangladesh, Nepal, China; southeastern Siberia, Myanmar (Burma), Vietnam, Laos, Thailand, and Sumatra

Status Population: 5,000–7,500; IUCN Endangered, CITES I. Previously hunted for fur and body parts, and to protect people and livestock

⊳ A Bengal tiger wades through water. Tigers are proficient swimmers and can cross rivers that are 4 to 5 miles (7 to 8 km) wide without difficulty.

⊳ Juvenile tigers are fond of play fighting like the two below.

20 SEE ALSO Lion 2:14; Boar, Wild 5:76; Deer and Relatives 6:10

A number of other features help you navigate through the volumes and present you with helpful extra information. At the bottom of many pages are **cross-references** to other articles of interest. They may be to related animals, animals that live in similar places, animals with similar behavior, predators (or prey), and much more. Each volume also contains a **Set Index** to the complete *World of Animals: Mammals*. All animals mentioned in the text are indexed by common and scientific names, and many topics are also covered. A **Glossary** will also help you if there are words used in the text that you do not fully understand. Each volume ends with a list of useful **Further Reading and Websites** that help you take your research further. Finally, under the heading "List of Species" you will find expanded listings of the animals that are covered in each volume.

Introductory article describes family or closely related groups

Detailed maps clarify animal's distribution

At-a-glance boxes cover topics of special interest

Meticulous drawings illustrate a typical selection of group members

Tables summarize classification of groups and give scientific names of animals mentioned in the text

Who's Who tables summarize classification of each major group and give scientific names of animals mentioned in the text

Introductory article describes major groups of animals

Graphic full-color photographs bring text to life

Detailed diagrams illustrate text

Find the Animal

World of Animals: Mammals is the first part of a library that describes all groups of living animals. Each cluster of volumes in *World of Animals* will cover a familiar group of animals—mammals, birds, reptiles and amphibians, fish, and insects and other invertebrates. These groups also represent categories of animals recognized by scientists (see The Animal Kingdom below).

The Animal Kingdom

The living world is divided into five kingdoms, one of which (kingdom Animalia) is the main subject of the *World of Animals*. Also included are those members of the kingdom Protista that were once regarded as animals, but now form part of a group that includes all single-cell organisms. Kingdom Animalia is divided into numerous major groups called Phyla, but only one of them (Chordata) contains those animals that have a backbone. Chordates, or vertebrates as they are popularly known, include all the animals familiar to us and those most studied by scientists—mammals, birds, reptiles, amphibians, and fish. In all, there are about 38,000 species of vertebrates, while the Phyla that contain animals without backbones (so-called invertebrates, such as insects, spiders, and so on) include at least 1 million species, probably many more. To find which set of volumes in the *World of Animals* is relevant to you, see the chart Main Groups of Animals (page 7).

Mammals in Particular

World of Animals: Mammals focuses on the most familiar of animals, those most easily recognized as having fur (although this may be absent in many sea mammals like whales and dolphins), and that provide milk for their young.

Mammals are divided into major groups (carnivores, primates, rodents, and marsupials to name just

The chart shows the major groups of mammals in this set arranged in evolutionary relationship (see page 10). The volume in which each group appears is indicated. You can find individual entries by looking at the contents page for each volume or by consulting the set index.

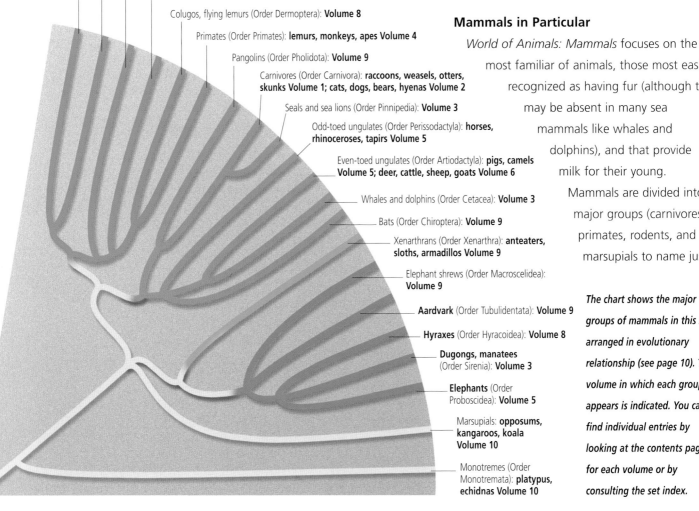

Rodents (Order Rodentia): **squirrels, rats, mice Volume 7; cavies, porcupines, chinchillas Volume 8**

Lagomorphs (Order Lagomorpha): **rabbits, hares, pikas Volume 8**

Tree shrews (Order Scandentia): **Volume 9**

Insectivores (Order Insectivora): **shrews, moles, hedgehogs Volume 9**

Colugos, flying lemurs (Order Dermoptera): **Volume 8**

Primates (Order Primates): **lemurs, monkeys, apes Volume 4**

Pangolins (Order Pholidota): **Volume 9**

Carnivores (Order Carnivora): **raccoons, weasels, otters, skunks Volume 1; cats, dogs, bears, hyenas Volume 2**

Seals and sea lions (Order Pinnipedia): **Volume 3**

Odd-toed ungulates (Order Perissodactyla): **horses, rhinoceroses, tapirs Volume 5**

Even-toed ungulates (Order Artiodactyla): **pigs, camels Volume 5; deer, cattle, sheep, goats Volume 6**

Whales and dolphins (Order Cetacea): **Volume 3**

Bats (Order Chiroptera): **Volume 9**

Xenarthrans (Order Xenarthra): **anteaters, sloths, armadillos Volume 9**

Elephant shrews (Order Macroscelidea): **Volume 9**

Aardvark (Order Tubulidentata): **Volume 9**

Hyraxes (Order Hyracoidea): **Volume 8**

Dugongs, manatees (Order Sirenia): **Volume 3**

Elephants (Order Proboscidea): **Volume 5**

Marsupials: **opposums, kangaroos, koala Volume 10**

Monotremes (Order Monotremata): **platypus, echidnas Volume 10**

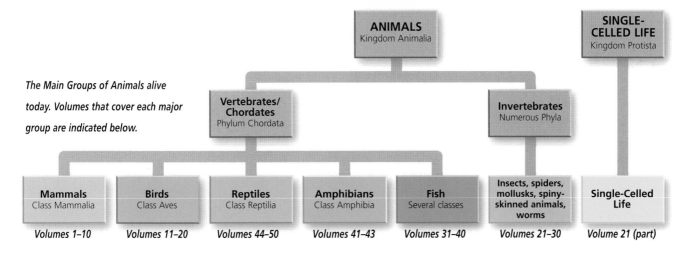

The Main Groups of Animals alive today. Volumes that cover each major group are indicated below.

| ANIMALS Kingdom Animalia | SINGLE-CELLED LIFE Kingdom Protista |

Vertebrates/Chordates Phylum Chordata

Invertebrates Numerous Phyla

| **Mammals** Class Mammalia | **Birds** Class Aves | **Reptiles** Class Reptilia | **Amphibians** Class Amphibia | **Fish** Several classes | Insects, spiders, mollusks, spiny-skinned animals, worms | **Single-Celled Life** |
| Volumes 1–10 | Volumes 11–20 | Volumes 44–50 | Volumes 41–43 | Volumes 31–40 | Volumes 21–30 | Volume 21 (part) |

a few). All the major groups are shown on the chart on page 6. To help you find particular animals, a few familiar ones, such as sheep, goats, cats, and dogs, have been included in the chart.

Naming Mammals

To be able to discuss animals, names are needed for the different kinds. Most people regard tigers as one kind of animal and lions as another. All tigers look more or less alike. They breed together and produce young like themselves. This popular distinction between kinds of animals corresponds closely to the zoologists' distinction between species. All tigers belong to one species and all lions to another. The lion species has different names in different languages (for example, *Löwe* in German, *Simba* in Swahili), and often a single species may have several common names. For example, the North American mountain lion is also known as the cougar, puma, panther, and catamount.

Zoologists find it convenient to have internationally recognized names for species and use a standardized system of two-word Latinized names. The lion is called *Panthera leo* and the tiger *Panthera tigris*. The first word, *Panthera*, is the name of the genus (a group of closely similar species), which includes the lion and the tiger. The second word, *leo* or *tigris*, indicates the particular species within the genus. Scientific names are recognized all over the world. The scientific name is used whatever the language, even where the alphabet is different, as in Chinese or Russian. The convention allows for precision and helps avoid most confusion. However, it is also common for one species to apparently have more than one scientific name. That can be because a particular

species may have been described and named at different times without the zoologists realizing it was one species.

It is often necessary to make statements about larger groups of animals: for example, all the catlike animals or all the mammals. A formal system of classification makes this possible. Domestic cats are similar to lions and tigers, but not as similar as those species are to each other (for example, they do not roar). They are put in a different genus (*Felis*), but *Felis*, *Panthera*, and other catlike animals are grouped together as the family Felidae. The flesh-eating mammals (cats, dogs, hyenas, weasels, and so on), together with a few plant-eaters that are obviously related to them (such as pandas), are grouped in the order Carnivora. These and all the other animals that suckle their young are grouped in the class Mammalia. Finally, the mammals are included, with all other animals that have backbones (fish, amphibians, reptiles, and birds) and some other animals that seem to be related to them, in the Phylum Chordata.

Rank	Scientific name	Common name
Phylum	Chordata	Animals with a backbone
Class	Mammalia	All mammals
Order	Carnivora	Flesh-eaters/carnivores
Family	Felidae	All cats
Genus	*Panthera*	Big cats
Species	*leo*	Lion

The kingdom Animalia is subdivided into phylum, classes, orders, families, genera, and species. Above is the classification of the lion.

PRIMATES

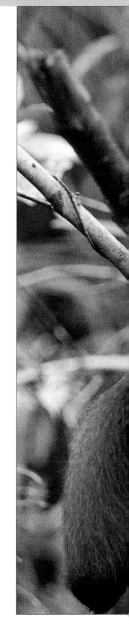

Apes, monkeys, lemurs, bush babies, and humans are all primates. They are an extremely diverse group of animals, exhibiting a wide range of colors, sizes, adaptations, and behaviors. The smallest living primate is the pygmy mouse lemur, which, at about 1 ounce (28 g), is only slightly larger than a house mouse. The largest is the western lowland gorilla—an adult male can weigh 330 pounds (150 kg).

Origins

Most of the physical features of primates are a result of their evolution as arboreal animals. In fact, many characteristics are shared with other unrelated tree creatures such as squirrels, tree shrews, and possums. They include a long back, a short, flexible neck, and forward-pointing eyes for stereoscopic vision—essential for judging distances when jumping between branches. Many primates, including most humans, have full-color vision, which is rare among mammals. A feature of male primates is a penis that hangs at the front rather than being tucked into the body, as in most other mammals.

Characteristics

One of the key characteristics of primates is the large, rounded skull. The face is usually flattened, with relatively short jaws. Most primates have a short nose, and their sense of smell is not as good as in many other mammals. Instead, they rely more heavily on their senses of sight, touch, and hearing. The large skull encases a huge brain. A large brain, and particularly a large neocortex (the part of the brain associated with creative thinking), is what gives primates the edge over other mammals in terms of intelligence. As well as processing all the sensory information coming from the eyes, nose, ears, and skin, primates use their brain to manage the complexities of their social lives. Many primates seem able to handle the mental jump associated with understanding how the world looks from another's perspective. That particular talent enables them to manipulate social situations and even deliberately deceive others in order to get their own way.

In all primates the hands and feet are good at grasping and clinging. The soles are hairless, and the palms and digits are padded. Many primates have opposable thumbs, with joints that are flexible enough to allow the thumb to bend across the palm of the hand to meet

a

b

Ⓚ *Skeletons of two primates: in the orangutan (a) the tail is absent, the back short, the rib cage broad, and the pelvis bones robust—features of a vertical posture. The guenon (b) shows the long back and narrow rib cage and pelvis—features of early primates. Primate hands and feet, showing structure adaptations to ways of life: spider monkey, showing reduced thumb for arm swinging (1); gibbon: thumb distant from fingers (2); gorilla: opposable thumb for precision gripping (3); macaque: hand adapted for walking on the ground (4); tamarin: clawed foot for branch running (5); siamang and orangutan: grasping big toe for climbing (6) and (7); baboon: long, slender foot for ground living (8).*

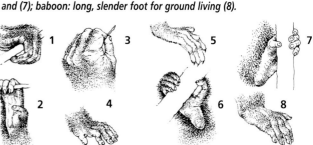

⬆ *A black uakari in the Brazilian rain forest. Together with the red uakari, it is the only short-tailed primate living in the New World. Most New World monkeys have long, prehensile tails (able to grasp).*

the fingers in a pinching motion. In all except humans the first toes are also opposable, making the feet also very good at grasping. The basic arboreal body plan is modified in different species according to where they live and how they move: Four limbs of roughly equal length is a common state. For primates that live in open forests with lots of upright tree trunks, the best way of getting around is jumping from trunk to trunk. Some bush babies do so and have extremely long legs for jumping. Long arms are excellent for swinging from branch to branch, as demonstrated by the great apes and gibbons. Slow,

careful climbers tend to have mobile joints and strong hands and feet. Agile branch runners, such as ring-tailed lemurs, need good balance. Their long tails, which they use as a counterweight, help achieve this.

Location and Lifestyle

Apart from humans, most primates live in the tropics or subtropics. They can be found in the Americas from Mexico to Argentina and Brazil. They are also found throughout most of Africa and Madagascar and in south-central and Southeast Asia as far east as Japan and Timor.

Typical habitat for primates is tropical forest, but some have colonized temperate forests, savanna, deserts, mountains, and coasts. Most are arboreal, but many spend much of their time on the ground.

Primate diets are variable. While some species specialize in eating insects, fruit, or leaves, most will supplement their diet with a range of items depending on availability. Chimps and baboons are known to hunt other animals, including other primates, and a few specialize in eating gum and resin from trees.

One of the most striking characteristics of primates is their sociability. Almost all primates live in groups, and social bonds tend to be long lasting. The main reason seems to be to avoid predators: In a group there are many eyes to look out for trouble, and with the force of numbers groups may be able to overpower a predator. There are even cases of baboons killing leopards. However, living in groups can be difficult if food is scarce, and large groups tend to occur where food is plentiful.

There are four basic group structures depending on species, season, and food availability: The mother and her offspring form the core of all groups. She may stick with a single male in a monogamous pair, as in gibbons. Otherwise she may forage alone within a male's territory that overlaps that of several females, as in orangutans. In colobus monkeys, guenons, and gorillas a small group of females (a harem) is guarded by a single male, who keeps other males away. Capuchin and howler monkeys live in large groups consisting of many males and females.

⊕ *Olive baboons take a rest break on the African savanna. When the baboon troop is resting, the animals may break into small subgroups of related individuals.*

Infanticide

One of the more unpleasant sides of primate life is the tendency of males to kill babies. In primate societies in which males compete for females a male has a strong drive to father as many offspring as possible in the short time he is top of the hierarchy. Mothers do not become ready to mate until they have finished nursing; so rather than wait, males sometimes kill babies fathered by another male to hasten the females back into fertility.

Humans as Primates

The latest biochemical evidence suggests that the split between humans and apes occurred between 5 and 10 million years ago in Africa. The earliest known hominid (humanlike animal) to be found is over 4 million years old. But we are close relatives, and sometimes apes and humans are placed in the same family, Hominidae.

Two physical features are key in human evolution: our large brains (larger compared with body size than for any other animal) and our ability to walk upright on two legs (known as bipedalism). Other animals use the upright posture occasionally, but none uses it as the normal means of travel. Walking upright left our ancestors' hands free for carrying and manipulating objects.

Tool use was once thought to be a uniquely human trait, but now many animals have been shown to use them. Even some birds are known to use sticks for picking

Chimpanzees are one species of primate that frequently use tools. The chimps use sticks to poke around in termite nests or employ bent sticks to pull down fruit-laden branches. Sticks are also used as weapons, levers, and even to clean teeth.

Higher and Lower Primates

There are over 230 species of primates in a dozen families. The families are divided into two groups. The first is the strepsirhines, or "lower primates," which include lemurs, pottos, and lorises. There are three main subgroups: bush babies from Africa; angwantibos, lorises, and pottos in the Old World, and the lemurs of Madagascar. There are no strepsirhines in America.

"Higher" primates, or haplorhines, include apes (and humans), monkeys, marmosets, and tamarins. The haplorhines are divided into two major groups: the platyrrhines and catarrhines.

Catarrhines are found in the Old World. They have close, narrow nostrils and hard pads on the buttocks for sitting (ischial callosities). The group includes the great apes, gibbons, Old World monkeys, and humans. Platyrrhines are only found in the New World. They have flat noses with wide-open nostrils that are far apart on the face. They also have prehensile tails. New World monkeys, tamarins, and marmosets are all platyrrhines.

Tarsiers have features of both groups, but the most up-to-date classifications list them with the haplorhines.

food from hard-to-reach places. However, no other animal uses the diversity of tools that humans do. Many animals make nests, beavers create dams, and termites build impressively tall, air-conditioned towers; but no other animal makes such drastic changes to its surroundings as we do. Humans have used creativity, adaptability, and inventiveness to spread across the entire world and even venture into space.

Unlike any other animal, humans have a spoken language with a large vocabulary and complex grammatical structure. Compared with the body language, calls, and chemical signaling used by other animals, speech is a superb way of communicating. Being able to describe past and future events, as well as describing situations from another's perspective (the basics of storytelling), is one of the most important characteristics of civilized human society.

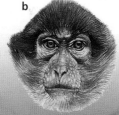

a

b

The terms catarrhine and platyrrhine come from the shape of the nose. Platyrrhines have nostrils that are wide open and far apart (a), while in catarrhines they are narrow and close together (b).

The Ape Family

The great apes are the closest living relatives of humans. Indeed, many scientists classify humans in the same zoological family as the great apes and call the family Hominidae. There is growing evidence from genetic and other molecular techniques that this is the best approach, since humans are more closely related to chimpanzees than chimpanzees are to orangutans. Yet humans are often put in a separate family to the apes.

What Is an Ape?

There are six species of great ape (seven if humans are included). The chimpanzees, bonobo, and gorillas live in equatorial Africa, while the orangutans live on the Indonesian islands of Sumatra and Borneo. All great apes are large, and most are bigger than humans. An adult western lowland gorilla stands at about 5.7 feet (1.7 m) tall and can weigh more than 330 pounds (150 kg). The largest ape ever to have lived was probably *Gigantopithecus*, which roamed Asia until the middle of the Pleistocene period, around 500,000 years ago. It stood between 8.2 and 9.8 feet (2.5 and 3 m) tall.

Apes have naked ears and faces. The face itself is very expressive, particularly in chimpanzees. Apes also have a barrel-shaped body compared with monkeys, whose bodies are flattened side-to-side. Apes have no tail, and all except humans have arms that are longer than their legs and hands and feet with opposable fingers and toes.

Family Hominidae: 7 species, including humans, in 4 genera	
Pan	2 species, common chimpanzee (*P. troglodytes*); bonobo (*P. paniscus*)
Pongo	2 species, Bornean orangutan (*P. pygmaeus*); Sumatran orangutan (*P. abelii*)
Gorilla	2 species, western gorilla (*G. gorilla*), including 2 subspecies western lowland gorilla (*G. g. gorilla*), Cross River gorilla (*G. g. diehli*); eastern gorilla (*G. beringei*), including 3 subspecies mountain gorilla (*G. b. beringei*), eastern lowland gorilla (*G. b. diehli*), and 1 unnamed subspecies
Homo	1 species, human (*H. sapiens*)

Apes generally move around on four limbs. Orangutans spend most of their time in trees, hanging from all four limbs and moving their great weight slowly and deliberately. The African apes tend to spend more time on the ground. Chimps and gorillas both "knuckle walk," curling their hands and putting their weight on their knuckles. None are known to swim.

Food and Feeding

Apes are predominantly vegetarian. Orangutans have a high proportion of fruit in their diet, while gorillas are largely leaf eaters. They all have large teeth (particularly the grinding molars) to process the huge amount of vegetable food needed to sustain their bulk. They also need large jaw muscles for all the heavy chewing. The jaw muscles are attached to a crest at the top of the skull. In male gorillas the crest becomes very large, giving them a characteristic high-crowned head shape. Chimpanzees and orangutans occasionally supplement their diet with meat. Chimps in particular will hunt medium-sized animals such as bush pigs and other primates, including red colobus monkeys and baboons. The males cooperate in hunting and will even share food. Interestingly, such examples of cooperation may have been the trigger for the evolution of humans.

Intelligence and Social Life

Brains in the great apes are large, even compared with other primates. The average brain capacity in chimpanzees is 24 cubic inches (394 cu. cm), 25 cubic inches (410 cu. cm) in orangutans, 31 cubic inches (508 cu. cm) in gorillas, and a massive 82 cubic inches (1,350 cu. cm) in humans. In the gibbons brain capacity is only around 6 cubic inches (95 cu. cm).

All apes appear to be highly intelligent. They are quick learners, picking up techniques from others in their group and from humans when they are in captivity. Although they do not use what we would call a

 SEE ALSO Orangutans 4:14; Gorilla, Mountain 4:20; Gorilla, Western Lowland 4:26; Chimpanzee 4:28; Bonobo 4:34

language, animals within a group clearly communicate with each other. In captivity chimpanzees and gorillas have been taught to use American Sign Language to exchange information with their human carers.

Of all the great apes, orangutans are the least social. The males avoid each other, but their territories do overlap those of several females. Gorillas live in a "harem," where around 12 females and young stay with one mature adult "silverback" male. Chimpanzees live in large, mixed-sex communities of 40 to 80 animals. They may disperse when feeding, but are highly territorial. Encounters with other groups can lead to deadly fights.

As in many species in which males have to compete for females, there is a strong selective pressure for males to grow larger. In gorillas and orangutans males are much larger than females. Reproductive cycles are very similar to

⊕ *A silverback eastern lowland gorilla resting. Oddly, the eastern lowland is less well known than its cousin, the mountain gorilla, despite the latter being fewer in numbers and inhabiting high altitudes.*

those of humans, and young are looked after by the mother for at least three years.

Experimental Tools

Apes are so similar to humans in their size, biochemistry, and other aspects of their biology that they have often been used to test drugs and surgical techniques. Often this was done with little consideration for animal welfare or for the conservation of species in the wild. However, the use of apes in biomedical research is much less common nowadays, and attempts have been made to return some laboratory apes to the wild.

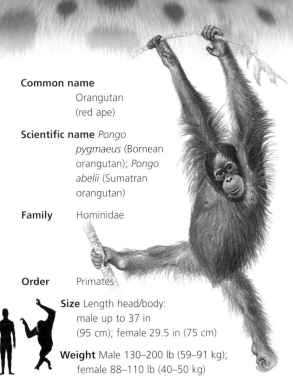

Common name
Orangutan
(red ape)

Scientific name *Pongo pygmaeus* (Bornean orangutan); *Pongo abelii* (Sumatran orangutan)

Family Hominidae

Order Primates

Size Length head/body: male up to 37 in (95 cm); female 29.5 in (75 cm)

Weight Male 130–200 lb (59–91 kg); female 88–110 lb (40–50 kg)

Key features Very long arms; feet are handlike; coat sparse and coarse, ranging from orange to dark brown

Habits Solitary; spends most of its time in treetops; active during the day, rests overnight in nests among branches

Breeding Single young born about every 8 years after gestation period of 8 months. Weaned at about 3 years; females sexually mature at 12 years, males at 15 years. May live 60 years in captivity, 45–50 in the wild

Voice Males make loud resonant calls with the help of their large throat pouches at a volume comparable to that of a lion's roar

Diet Fruit (such as mangoes and figs), young shoots, bark, and insects

Habitat Lowland and hilly tropical rain forest

Distribution Confined to the islands of Sumatra (Indonesia) and lowland Borneo

Status Population: about 20,000; IUCN Endangered; CITES I. Forest clearance is biggest threat

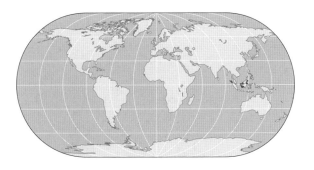

Orangutans

Pongo pygmaeus
and *P. abelii*

Orangutans are Asia's only great apes. Their shaggy, reddish coats make them one of the most distinctive of all mammals. Despite their considerable size, they spend most of their lives high up in the treetops.

FOSSIL REMAINS INDICATE that the magnificent orangutan once ranged throughout southern Asia from the foothills of the Himalayas to southern China. Nowadays, orangutans are confined to the tropical rain forests of northern Sumatra (Indonesia) and the low-lying swamps of Borneo (a large island shared between Indonesia and Malaysia). Orangutans are the largest tree-living animals in the world. In fact, their name comes from the Malay words *orang*, meaning "man," and *utan*, meaning "forest"— so literally "man of the forest." It is a good description, since orangs are never found anywhere except among dense, tall trees.

Asian Apes

Even at first glance there are obvious differences between orangutans and other great apes, such as chimpanzees and gorillas. They are the only non-African apes, and their shaggy appearance bears little resemblance to that of their African cousins. Their bright reddish color again makes them distinct from all other apes and most monkeys too. Orangs are also generally solitary, while other apes (and most other primates) live in social groups.

There are two distinct types of orangs, one type found on Sumatra and the other on Borneo. Analysis of their DNA (genetic molecular structure) suggests that the two populations became separated around 1.5 million years ago. Since then the orangutans of each island have evolved and developed separately in their different environments to the extent that they are now considered to be two distinctly different species. Until recently they were considered as two subspecies of a single species. Generally, the Sumatran orangutans are

SEE ALSO Gorilla, Mountain **4:**20; Gorilla, Western Lowland **4:**26; Chimpanzee **4:**28

A young Sumatran orangutan. The young of the species are more sociable than their elders and may join together to play or even travel around in pairs. Older animals are more solitary.

lighter in color and have thicker and longer hair than those in Borneo. The difference may be due to the cooler conditions in Sumatra, where the orangs live at higher altitudes.

Males of both races develop impressive flaps of skin on either side of the face. They are called cheek flanges and make the male orang's face appear very broad and almost circular. They are a conspicuous feature of any adult male orangutan, making it look quite different from any other species of primate. The flanges seem to serve no obvious practical function, except as a symbol of rank and status. The cheek flange is another way in which the orangs of the two islands differ: The flanges start to develop at about eight years of age in the Bornean orangutans. The Sumatran males are late developers, and their flanges do not appear until about the age of 10. The flanges of the Borneo males grow outward and forward from the head, resulting in a round, dishlike shape to the face. They stop growing around the age of 15. In contrast, the flanges of the Sumatran orangutan do not complete their development until the animal is about 20 years of age. Their cheeks also only grow sideways, rather than forward, giving the Sumatran male a much flatter-looking face.

Novelty Value

Despite its size, the orangutan was completely unknown to science and the western world until the 17th century. The first live orangutan arrived in Europe in 1776 and caused quite a stir, since it was so different from any animal seen before. It was also strikingly similar to a human, exciting considerable comment and interest concerning the relationship between humans and the animal world.

The orangutan has a large, bulky body, a thick neck, and short, bowed legs. The arms are very long and immensely strong. The hands of an orangutan are much like our own, with four fingers and a thumb that can press against them. That arrangement enables the orangs to grasp food and other objects—and the orang's

long fingers to get a tight grip on branches. Orangutans can suspend their whole weight from just a couple of fingers without getting tired. Their feet are similar to their hands, only longer with an opposable big toe. That enables the orang to grasp objects with its feet as well as its hands when moving through trees.

Fruit Eaters

The jaws of the red ape are massive, and they have large teeth covered in thick enamel, ideal for their feeding habits. They are essentially vegetarian, but they have been known to feed on animal material such as insects, birds, and small mammals. Their diet consists mainly of soft fruits like mangoes and figs, but they also feed on leaves, tree bark, and seeds. They are especially fond of large durian fruits that smell strongly when they are ripe. Orangs will travel long distances through the forest to visit favorite feeding trees when their fruits are in season. Orangutans are important for rain-forest plants because they disperse seeds throughout the forest in their droppings. Also, by choosing to eat green leaves and shoots, they stimulate further plant growth.

The orangutan is almost entirely arboreal. Because females are much smaller than males, they are at greater risk from predators such as tigers when on the ground. Consequently, they

⊕ *Orangutans are the only truly arboreal ape. They are the largest animal that lives in the forest canopy, sleeping in "nests" made from twigs and leaves high up in the treetops.*

spend nearly all their time in the treetops. Because of their size orangs will rarely walk on top of branches or jump from one branch to another the way smaller monkeys do. Instead, they hang by their powerful arms. They can swing with breathtaking speed from branch to branch using both their hands and feet. When they are traveling among thin branches or arrive at a gap between trees, they will reach out, catch onto the tip of a branch in the next tree, and haul it in until they have grasped it well enough to transfer their weight. If the gap is too wide to reach across, they start to swing, hanging by their arms and slowly building up momentum like a pendulum. Finally, a swing takes them far enough to reach the next branch. Young orangs often find it difficult to cross the gaps, and so mothers may hold branches together to help the youngsters scramble across. A female orangutan may even create a bridge out of her own body to allow her baby to get from one branch to another.

Nests in the Trees

Orangutans are diurnal and usually go to bed at sunset, around 7 PM. They sleep in a nest, which they construct every evening, although they may also build nests during the day in which to rest and play. Favored areas for nesting face westward toward the sunset and are sometimes

Quick Learners

Orangutans are highly intelligent. Wild orangs rely on their mental prowess to develop complex feeding techniques, sometimes involving the use of tools. Orangutans are also excellent mimics. As a result, skills are quickly passed on from one individual to another. Groups in particular areas have even developed their own local traditions in the way they build nests and feed. Orangs can also learn from humans, and certain individuals in captivity have been taught to use American Sign Language. That enables them to communicate with people and reveals a capability to learn words and perform tasks when told to do so. Their mental abilities are similar to those of a three-year-old child.

Endangered Orangs

Orangutans have a few natural predators, such as tigers and clouded leopards, but nevertheless they have become rare. Humans are a much more serious threat. Large numbers of young orangs used to be captured and kept as pets or exported to zoos. Often the adult females were shot in order to take the babies, effectively removing two animals instead of just one. In addition, slow breeding in the species means that lost animals cannot be replaced quickly.

Consequently, the orangutan has become scarce. There are now effective controls on international trade, and strict protection has reduced the threat posed by the collection of live animals. Moreover, zoos are now able to breed orangs successfully, so there is no need to take more from the wild. Programs have been developed to help confiscated pet orangs readjust to the wild, and there are sanctuaries where rescued animals have been released back into the forests.

However, throughout Borneo and Sumatra there is a continuing problem of human expansion into forested areas. The deliberate starting of forest fires claims the land for agricultural use. Trees are cut down for fuel and for the construction of houses for a human population that continues to grow. Logging has removed huge areas of orang habitat and threatens still more. The remaining patches of forest are often too small to support viable populations, which need a lot of space. The orangutan is therefore classified by the IUCN as an Endangered species, but it is unlikely to die out completely because it now breeds well in captivity. It may also survive in a few protected reserves. However, everywhere else the future for this unique and fascinating animal looks bleak.

above water, helping reduce the dangers posed by nocturnal predators. The nests are made out of soft twigs and leaves, and are woven into the branches of a tree like a big basket. They can reach 3 feet (1 m) across. Baby orangutans are born in the nests, which can be about 90 feet (30 m) above ground level. Fully grown males are restricted to nesting lower down, where the tree branches are thicker and can take their greater weight.

Orangs live alone in large territories. The longest bond between individuals is that between a mother and her offspring. It is thought that the orangs' solitary nature may be because of their feeding habits: They need a large area to get enough food because not all the trees will have ripe fruits at the same time. Too many individuals sharing the area might result in all the suitable fruits being eaten at once, leading to starvation. Apart from the early relationship between a mother and its dependent young, there is little close interaction

A female orangutan with a nine-month-old youngster. Young are reared solely by their mother. Sumatran males will remain with their mate until the birth.

between orangutans, and they spend the majority of their lives entirely alone.

Male orangutans are capable of making very long, loud calls that carry for over half a mile through the forest. The call is unique to orangutans and is made up of a series of loud roars followed by a bellow. A large, resonating throat pouch amplifies the sound to a volume comparable with that of a lion's roar. Male orangs in Borneo have a larger throat pouch than their Sumatran relatives and so are capable of emitting the loudest sounds. Calling helps the male claim his territory by warning off other males in the surrounding forest. It may also help him find a mate. Without such calls it would be difficult for orangs to locate each other in the dense forest.

Competing Calls

A male's territory is important because it contains both food and females. By making loud territorial calls, the males can avoid the dangers and effort involved in fighting over access to precious resources. The better the call, the more likely the male is to succeed in staking out his territory and attracting a mate. Each male's territory is generally large enough to include the areas used by about four females. A female that already has a young infant will climb to the top of the trees to avoid contact with the calling male. He will not follow her into the thin branches that cannot take his weight. The call is a display of the male's size and status. The females will assess the calls and

choose the best-sounding male with whom to mate. On Borneo the male/female relationships are only likely to last two days at the most, while Sumatran males often stay near their partner as a bodyguard until the young are born. Heavily pregnant females are less able to defend themselves against predators such as the tiger. That may be important in Sumatra because of the greater dangers lurking in the rain forest there.

A pregnant female will have to compete with other species for food, and this becomes more and more difficult in the later stages of her pregnancy. A large, strong male can aid her through this difficult time. For that reason a female Sumatran orangutan is very selective about whom she will mate with; it may be why males in Sumatra engage in displays of physical prowess to impress females. The strange displays involve calling and hanging upside down from high branches. The female uses these displays to assess the strength and stamina of the male and his chances of being able to defend her. Active displays seem to be less frequent among Bornean orangutans.

Orangs are extremely slow breeders, and the average age for a wild female orangutan to give birth to her first offspring is about 15 years old. In fact, in her lifetime a female orangutan can only expect to rear at most four surviving young, which is one of the slowest reproductive rates of all mammals. In the first year of a baby's life its mother will carry it almost continuously. Until it is about four years old, whenever the mother is on the move, the young orangutan will be carried. The young are generally more sociable than their elders. Juveniles may join together and engage in play for a few hours or even travel around in pairs. Once they become adolescent, the males may break away from their mother and go to live somewhere else. Young females, on the other hand, often remain nearby.

A Bornean male orangutan, showing his large facial flaps. The flanges seem to serve no obvious practical function, except as a symbol of rank and status.

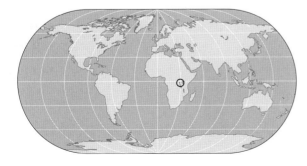

Common name Mountain gorilla (eastern gorilla)

Scientific name *Gorilla beringei beringei*

Family	Hominidae
Order	Primates
Size	Height (standing upright): male 4.6–5.9 ft (1.4–1.8 m); female 4.3–5 ft (1.3–1.5 m); arm span: 7.5 ft (2.3 m)
	Weight Male up to 400 lb (181 kg); female up to 200 lb (90 kg)
Key features	Large, bulky ape with barrel-shaped body; muscular arms longer than legs; coat blue-black, turning gray with age, males with silver patch on back; hair short on back, long elsewhere; broad face and massive jaws
Habits	Social groups of 5–30 animals centered around 1 (or occasionally 2) dominant "silverback" male; docile, spends most time feeding or resting; males display their strength by chest-beating and plant-thrashing
Breeding	Usually 1 infant born every 4 years after gestation period of 250–270 days. Weaned at 2.5–3 years; females sexually mature at 8–10 years, males at 10 years. May live 35 years
Voice	Howling, roaring, grunting, and snarling
Diet	Leaves, stems, berries, roots, pulp, and bark
Habitat	Montane rain forest and subalpine scrub at altitudes of 5,400–12,400 ft (1,645–3,780 m)
Distribution	Borders of Democratic Republic of Congo, Rwanda, and Uganda
Status	Population: about 320; IUCN Critically Endangered; CITES I. Most threatened gorilla species

Mountain Gorilla

Gorilla beringei beringei

Mountain gorillas are gentle giants. They live in peaceful groups with a single dominant male. Of the five subspecies of gorilla, the mountain gorilla is the most studied and perhaps the most threatened.

MOUNTAIN GORILLAS LIVE IN a small area of the volcanic Virunga mountain range on the borders of Rwanda, Uganda, and Democratic Republic of Congo. High in the mountains the rain forest is almost always cloudy and cold, even though it is near the equator. Occasionally, the gorillas venture even higher into the alpine meadows at 13,100 feet (4,000 m), where temperatures fall well below freezing at night.

Dominating Presence

Gorillas are huge. Females weigh around twice as much as an average person, and the males weigh twice as much as the females. The only other animals that gorillas could be confused with are chimpanzees, but gorillas are much bigger and bulkier than chimps.

Mountain gorillas have long black fur to keep them warm in the cold, wet mountains. The hair on the back of a mature male gorilla is gray, hence the name of "silverback." Mountain gorillas have a broad, hairless face, small ears, nostrils banded by a wide ridge that extends to the upper lip, and massive jaws. They need big jaw muscles to chew the tough plant material that they eat. There is a ridge on the skull that the jaw muscles are attached to. In males the ridge and the jaw muscles are huge and give the head a characteristic bulge. Males also have long and robust canine teeth. Gorillas, especially the males, need to spend a lot of time eating to maintain their huge bulk. They eat a wide range of plants, including wild celery, nettles, wild cherry, bamboo, and thistles. As well as leaves, they will also crunch up bark, coarse stems, roots, and vines. In the

⬇ *A female mountain gorilla eating spiny leaves: These gentle giants are exclusively vegetarian. A mountain gorilla's diet is mainly made up of leaves, stems, roots, and other types of vegetation, but rarely fruit.*

mountains where they live, there is not much fruit, but they love to eat berries when they are available. They will eat fungi and some insects such as ants, but such small items are hardly worth the bother. They use their hands when they eat to pick plants and strip bark from stems to reach the succulent pith inside.

Laid-back Lifestyle

Gorillas are very docile animals. They are active during the day and spend about a third of the daytime resting, when the group gathers around the silverback male. They sleep or peacefully groom each other while the youngsters play.

They usually move slowly and spend most of their time on the ground. They mostly walk on all fours, with their hands curled into fists so they walk on their knuckles. They are able to climb trees, but the huge males are too heavy for all except the largest lower branches to support their weight. Only the young animals are light and agile enough to swing through the thinner branches high up.

Every night each animal builds a nest to sleep in by bending branches to make a comfortable, springy platform.

Gorilla Groupings—Species and Subspecies

Gorillas live only in equatorial Africa. There are two species, the western gorilla (*Gorilla gorilla*) and eastern gorilla (*Gorilla beringei*). They are divided into five subspecies.

There are three subspecies of eastern gorilla: the mountain gorilla (*G. beringei beringei*), which lives on the borders of Democratic Republic of Congo (DRC), Uganda, and Rwanda; the eastern lowland gorilla (*G. b. diehli*), which lives in the eastern central region of DRC; and another (unnamed) subspecies from the Bwindi Impenetrable Forest in Uganda.

Of the western gorillas the most common is the western lowland gorilla (*G. gorilla gorilla*). The Cross River gorilla (*G. g. diehli*), which lives along the border of Nigeria and Cameroon, has recently been classed as a separate subspecies and is Critically Endangered.

The nests are either in trees, on steep slopes, or on the ground. Since each gorilla makes its own nest, researchers can count the nests to ascertain how many animals are in a group even after they have left the area.

Despite their fierce reputation from films such as *King Kong*, gorillas have a quiet temperament and are very gentle unless they are threatened. They will let people get close to them as long as they sit quietly and do not stare. Staring is seen as a threat in gorilla society. If threatened, a male will protect his group, first with a display of strength and then by attacking fiercely.

Gorilla Society

Because mountain gorillas feed mainly on leaves, which are plentiful and available all year round, they can live in large groups without taking the risk of running out of food. The same animals stay with the group for months or years. There are usually between five and 10 animals in a group, but there can be up to 30 or 40. Groups are not territorial: Their feeding ranges often overlap, but their loud calls let other groups know where they are, so they avoid direct contact.

A large silverback male leads each group. He decides where the group will feed each day, protects them from danger, and usually fathers all the offspring. If the leading male dies, a younger male will quickly take over. As well as the silverback, there will usually be one or two subadult "blackback" males, several adult females, and up to 10 infants in one group.

Females nearly always leave their mother's group when they become sexually mature. This is unusual in primates, but prevents inbreeding. If a female stayed in the group, she would mate with the dominant male. He would be her father, or if he had died, a cousin, since one of his sons usually takes over. The offspring of such matings are usually not as healthy as those from matings between unrelated animals.

A female leaving a group will head straight to a nearby solitary male, but she does not necessarily stay with him. She probably chooses

⊕ *After feeding, mountain gorilla groups—like the one above—gather around the silverback to rest in the middle of the day. Females with infants (1) move closest to the silverback (2), while females without young stay farther in the background (3). The juveniles will play close to the silverback under his protective gaze (4), but subadult males are merely tolerated (5).*

a male according to the quality of the habitat in his home range and his fighting ability. Such matters are important if he is to protect her and her offspring from predators and other males.

Although groups are stable, it is each female's contact with the leading male, rather than with each other, that keeps them together. Bonds between the dominant male and the females, and females and their offspring, are maintained by mutual grooming. However, it is rare to see social grooming between mature females that are not close relatives.

When young males mature, at 11 to 13 years old, around half leave the group that they were born in. A male may choose to stay with the group if there are too many mature females for the dominant male to mate with alone or if the dominant male is old. If they leave, young males spend time on their own or with a small group of other bachelor males before starting their own harem, usually by luring females away from an established group.

If the leader of a group is threatened by a solitary male, he asserts his dominance with a show of strength. He roars loudly, draws himself up to his full height, and beats his chest with his hands. Then he rushes toward the intruder, tearing up bushes and small trees. Such behavior is a big bluff, designed to intimidate a rival and avoid a fight. Fights between males are rare; but when they do

Studying Mountain Gorillas

The mountain gorillas have been studied very closely for many years. Dian Fossey was one famous researcher who lived with the gorillas. Researchers allow the gorillas to get used to their presence by spending a lot of time just hanging out with them. The process is called "habituation." Once the gorillas are used to people, they behave normally, and the researchers can study them without causing disturbance.

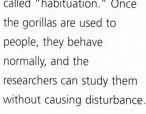

⬆ Despite their size, mountain gorillas are really gentle giants. They will tolerate people as long as they do not stare, which the gorilla's regard as a threat.

happen, they can be extremely fierce. The animals' long canine teeth can cause serious wounds and sometimes even death.

Competition between males is one reason why they are so large compared with the females and have much bigger canine teeth. Bigger males are more likely to succeed in scaring away rivals with their displays or to win a fight. A successful male gorilla may father 10 to 20 offspring over a 50-year life span. Unsuccessful males may never mate at all.

Caring for Young

Female gorillas become sexually mature at about six to eight years old, but they will not have their first baby until they have joined a stable group, usually around the age of 10. Gorillas will mate at any time of the year. Gestation lasts for about eight and a half months, after which a single baby is born. Twins are very rare; and because they are so difficult to look after, one of them usually dies.

At birth, a baby gorilla is almost bald and weighs about 4 pounds (1.8 kg), around half the weight of a human baby. At first it is carried by its mother, who holds it to her tummy. After a few weeks it can hang onto its mother's long chest fur by itself. Older babies ride on their mother's back. They start to eat solid food at

3

5

4

around three years; but they will stay with their mother, sleep in her nest, and drink her milk until the age of four to five years.

Many baby gorillas die young, so a mother may only rear one offspring to reproductive age every eight years. The slow reproduction rate means that gorilla populations take a long time to recover from losses.

Future Threats

Mountain gorillas are Critically Endangered animals. There are only about 300 of them left, and these remaining few are under pressure from hunting and a shrinking habitat. Although most of the area where the gorillas live is protected as a national park, people trespass on their habitat, chop down the trees, and build houses right up to and even inside the park boundary. Gorillas are also threatened by poachers (illegal hunters), who use guns or snares to kill the animals. Most snares are made of a wire loop connected to a rope tied to a bent bamboo pole. When an animal steps into the wire loop, the bamboo springs back and pulls the wire tight around its leg or neck, trapping it painfully. Snares are particularly dangerous to baby gorillas because they are inquisitive and will investigate anything new.

⊖ *Male mountain gorillas are twice the size of females. Their huge bulk and the low nutritional content of their food mean they must spend much of their time feeding.*

Gorillas and Guerillas

In recent years the countries where the mountain gorillas live have been in conflict. During war saving gorillas is not the highest priority for local people, and their governments are too poor to protect the animals. There are not enough park wardens, and it is a dangerous job because guerillas (members of unofficial armies) use the forest to hide in. Some gorillas have been shot accidentally, and the guerillas also kill the animals to eat.

Common name Western lowland gorilla

Scientific name *Gorilla gorilla gorilla*

Family Hominidae

Order Primates

Size Height: male about 5.5 ft (1.7 m), occasionally up to 5.9 ft (1.8 m); female 5 ft (1.5 m); arm span: 7.5 ft (2.3 m)

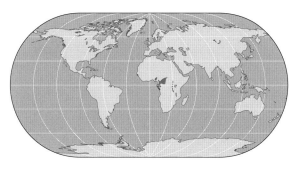

    Weight Male 310–450 lb (140–204 kg); female 200 lb (90 kg)

Key features Largest primate with bulky body and arms longer than legs; coat relatively short and brown to dark gray; mature males have silver-gray back; broad face with fairly small jaws

Habits Lives in small groups of 4 to 8 animals, with 1 dominant "silverback" male; active during the day, nights spent in nests; docile, spends around a third of the day resting

Breeding Usually 1 young born every 4 years after gestation period of 250–270 days. Weaned at 2.5–3 years; females sexually mature at 6–8 years, males at 8–10 years. May live about 50 years in captivity, 35 in the wild

Voice Roars, growls, barks, grunts, purrs, croaks, hoots, squeaks, and screeches

Diet Fruit, seeds, leaves, plant stems, bark, and invertebrates such as termites and caterpillars

Habitat Swamp and tropical forest

Distribution Central-western Africa

Status Population: fewer than 50,000; IUCN Endangered; CITES I. Vulnerable to poaching and habitat loss

Western Lowland Gorilla

Gorilla gorilla gorilla

The western lowland gorilla is the commonest of the gorillas and is the species that is often kept in zoos. However, hardly anyone has studied them in the wild.

WESTERN LOWLAND GORILLAS are similar to mountain gorillas in their basic body plan, with a huge bulky body and long arms. Their feet and hands are broad with stubby fingers, since they spend most of the time on the ground, moving around by "knuckle-walking." Western lowland gorillas have shorter fur than mountain gorillas, since they live in warmer areas. Their fur is browner, and their faces are broad with smaller jaws. One of the best ways of telling the two species apart is by looking at their nose—lowland gorillas have an overhanging tip.

Western lowland gorillas are found in the African countries of Cameroon, Congo, Gabon, Central African Republic, Democratic Republic of Congo, and Equatorial Guinea. Their population numbers a few tens of thousands of animals. Although they are much more common than mountain gorillas, their behavior in the wild is not nearly as well studied.

The Cross River gorilla (*G. gorilla diehli*) was recently recognized as a distinct subspecies. It lives in small pockets of habitat on the Cameroon-Nigeria border and is Critically Endangered, with only 120 to 150 animals left.

Forest Feeding

Western lowland gorillas live in dense primary forest that has never been cut down. They will also use secondary forests (where trees grow again after the original forest has been removed). Secondary forests tend to be less diverse and frequently offer less food than the original forest cover, but the gorillas can manage there nevertheless. Hence they are less threatened by forest removal than many less adaptable species. They are also found in

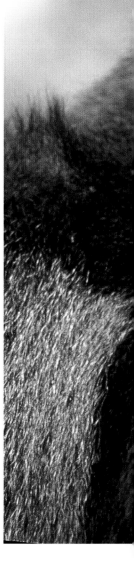

Lowland gorillas eat more fruit than mountain gorillas. They also eat insects such as termites, which they "fish" for, using twigs that they poke into termite nests.

lowland swamps and montane forests up to altitudes of 10,000 feet (3,000 m). Because of their huge size gorillas are not very good at climbing trees, so they prefer areas where thick vegetation grows near the ground. Such conditions are often found in clearings on the edges of the forest.

Lowland gorillas have a social structure similar to mountain gorillas, with each group being led by a "silverback" male. Group sizes are smaller than in mountain gorillas, with four to eight mature animals.

As with mountain gorillas, the males are very protective of their group. Intruders are deterred by noisy displays of howling and chest-beating. The male then charges at the intruder, crashing through the vegetation and ripping up bushes and small trees. In the swampy forests of the Congo Basin males even use water in their displays. They jump into pools and splash huge plumes of water with their hands.

Captive Gorillas

If you see a gorilla in a zoo, it will be a lowland gorilla. There are no mountain gorillas in zoos. Some western lowland gorillas have been taught to communicate with humans by using American Sign Language. Gorillas have learned vocabularies of hundreds of words; some can even string words together into simple phrases.

Although lowland gorillas are relatively common, their future is uncertain. The forests where they live are under pressure as people cut down the trees for timber and firewood and to make space for agriculture and houses. Gorillas are also hunted. Their heads and hands are cut off to be sold as "fetishes" or charms, or as grisly souvenirs for tourists. Gorilla meat is also a favorite in some areas.

In many areas deforestation and the bushmeat trade are interlinked. Logging companies build roads into areas that were previously difficult to get to. Poachers can easily reach the animals as a result. The workers employed to fell the trees need to eat, so poachers have a good market for gorilla meat.

Common name Chimpanzee

Scientific name *Pan troglodytes*

Family	Hominidae
Order	Primates

Size Length head/body: male 27.5–35 in (70–89 cm); female 25–33 in (63–84 cm); height: 39–66 in (99–168 cm)

Weight Male 75–154 lb (34–70 kg); female 57–110 lb (26–50 kg)

Key features Coat brownish or black, graying with age; face bare and brownish pink

Habits Active during the day, nights spent in platform nests in trees; usually seen in groups; generally travels on ground, sometimes walks upright, but usually on all fours using knuckles of hands

Breeding Single young born every 5 or 6 years after gestation period of about 230 days. Weaned at 3.5–4.5 years; sexually mature at around 7 years, but females do not breed until aged 14–15, males at 15–16 years. May live up to 60 years in captivity, similar in the wild

Voice Wide range of calls, including hoots, barks, grunts, and screams

Diet Varied; includes fruit, flowers, seeds, bark, insects, birds' eggs, and meat

Habitat Deciduous, montane, and tropical rain forests; also patchy savanna woodland

Distribution Western and central Africa

Status Population: 150–230,000; IUCN Vulnerable; CITES I. Threatened due to deforestation

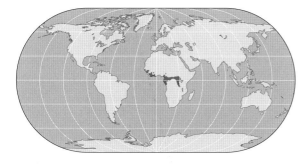

Chimpanzee

Pan troglodytes

Chimps are close relatives of humans. They are intelligent and adaptable, and learn quickly how to exploit new situations. The animals lead complex social lives, with each individual having its own distinct personality.

CHIMPS LIVE IN LARGE GROUPS known as communities. A community can have up to 120 animals, but they are rarely all together at once. They spend time on their own or in small groups. One day they might be hunting with a large gang, the next foraging in a smaller group with different individuals, and the next sneaking off with a partner. Females tend to spend more time on their own or with their offspring, while the males are more sociable.

Knowing Your Place

Hierarchy is very important in chimp society. The dominant male often has three high-ranking males as aides, with other males forming a constantly shifting power network among the subordinate animals. A hierarchy exists among females too, but it is less important and less vigorously fought over. In chimp communities rank is not inherited as in many other primate societies, but has to be earned and maintained by constant effort. Hierarchy positions can change with an animal's health, strength, and the influence of his friends.

Bonds between animals are very important. The strongest are between a mother and her offspring, and may last for the mother's lifetime. Males make strong friendships with each other. Having friends that will back them up in fights is a good way of defending their position within the hierarchy. While a male on his own may not be strong enough to challenge a higher-ranking male, together two males may be more successful. Close alliances can be more important than strength and bullying tactics in chimpanzee society.

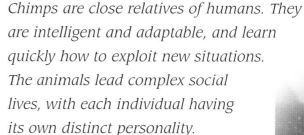

SEE ALSO Orangutans **4:**14; Gorilla, Mountain **4:**20; Gorilla, Western Lowland **4:**26; Bonobo **4:**34

Chimps as Doctors

Chimps sometimes eat soil to aid the digestion of plants that contain toxins. They also eat plants for medicinal purposes: Chimps occasionally eat *Aspilia*—a plant with very rough leaves. They usually eat it first thing in the morning and in a very different way than normal food. They choose each leaf carefully, holding the leaves between their lips and rejecting some but eating others. They do not chew the leaves, but roll them around in their mouth before swallowing. Some African people also use *Aspilia* for stomach complaints, and it has antibiotic and antiparasitic properties. It is thought that chimps use *Aspilia* to remove intestinal worms.

Females do not tend to make such close friendships as males. The most important thing for them is to secure a good area in which to live. They tend to rely on their family members to support them, rather than on friends. A female's rank is therefore highly dependent on how many offspring she has.

Home Ranges

Each community of chimpanzees has its own home range. The size depends on the number of animals in the group and the quality of the habitat (especially the amount of food available in it). In a good rain forest with lots of fruiting trees the area a group uses will vary from 2 to 15.5 square miles (5 to 40 sq. km), averaging about 5 square miles (13 sq. km). In open savanna country, where good fruit and nesting trees are scarce, chimps need a larger range. In one savanna community in Senegal 30 chimps ranged over an area of 129 square miles (334 sq. km).

Animals know their home range well and have a "mental map" of the network of paths within it. They remember where to find fruiting trees, and when the fruit is likely to be ripe. When they go foraging, they do not move randomly, but use their knowledge of the area

⊕ *A male chimpanzee eating harungana berries in the Mahale Mountains, Tanzania. Chimpanzees eat a huge range of foods, although around 60 percent of their diet consists of fruit. They also consume meat and will kill monkeys and other mammals.*

Friendships are maintained by grooming, hugging, kissing, and patting on the back. Hugging and kissing are seen more often between male chimps than between females. Animals spend many hours grooming each other, removing dirt and parasites from the fur, and cleaning wounds. As well as being physically beneficial, grooming has an important social function: It is used to strengthen friendships, patch up quarrels, confirm dominance, and to exchange favors.

↑ *The chimpanzee has a more varied repertoire of facial expressions than any other mammal except humans. The play face (1) is characterized by an open mouth and concealed teeth; threat display face used during an attack (2); pout used for begging for food (3); full grin, showing intense fear or excitement (4); submissive pout (5); and fear grin, used to approach a higher-ranking animal (6).*

↓ *A chimpanzee group in Tanzania. Groups are territorial and protect their home ranges with loud calls, threats, and even physical violence.*

to search in likely places. Each day is planned so that not only are they more likely to come across food, but they will also not be too far away from nesting trees at night or from places to drink. Remembering where streams are is particularly important in the dry season.

Females, particularly those with young, do not travel as far as the males. They stick to their own "core ranges" and may only travel 1 or 2 miles (1.6 to 3 km) per day. Males can easily trek 4 miles (6.4 km) in a day and may explore the whole of their home range. In doing so, they overlap with the ranges of several females.

Tribal Warfare

Chimpanzees are territorial and protect their home ranges from other chimp communities using noisy threat displays and physical assaults. Groups of males patrol the borders of their range and use loud calls to announce their presence. When two groups from different communities meet, there is usually a display of strength that only rarely ends in actual fighting. Occasionally, males will mount deliberate invasions of another group's range. They have been

known to carry out raids, repeatedly entering another group's territory, hunting and killing individual members until the entire group is wiped out. Such behavior is strikingly similar to tribal warfare in humans and is not known in any other type of animal.

Communication between group members is vital if they are to maintain social bonds, reaffirm positions in the social hierarchy, announce food discoveries, and alert others to leopards and other threats. Communication is both vocal and visual. Chimps use a wide variety of calls, including barks, contented "hooing" and lip-smacking, sociable grunts, loud "pant-hoots," and also piercing screams. Sound is an important way of staying in contact when groups are in dense forest and cannot see each other. When animals are within sight, sounds are usually accompanied by postures and facial expressions. Their naked faces and large, muscular lips give chimpanzees very expressive faces on which emotions and messages can be easily read. A wide-open mouth with the lips covering the teeth is a "play face." Chimps use the expression during play or to encourage a game. In contrast, an open mouth with lips pulled back to expose the teeth and gums is a "fear grin," showing anxiety and distress.

Posturing is important in communicating rank and acceptance. A dominant male maintains his position by his behavior, using displays of strength in which he charges around screaming and throwing branches. With his fur standing on end he makes himself look even larger. A subordinate, lower-ranking animal will behave submissively to him. With fur laid flat he darts to and fro in front of the dominant male, panting and screaming, then turns his back and crouches or bobs up and down. The dominant male acknowledges the submissive male with a hand on his back to reassure him.

Drum Beating

Vocal noises will also be supplemented by beating trees like a drum. The large, flat buttress roots of many tropical forest trees reverberate when hit with the fists: Male chimps often use the trees to send throbbing signals echoing through the forest to other members of their group.

Chimpanzees eat an enormous range of foods. At least 60 percent of their diet is ripe fruit. They also eat leaves, seeds, and other plant parts. Insects, especially termites, are an important source of protein and so are birds' eggs. Chimps also like to steal honey from bees and will eat over 20 different types of insects. Their identification skills are better than most human naturalists', and they select food from among 150 to 200 different plants, recognizing the edible ones from the many other poisonous or inedible species in the forest.

Chimps also eat meat. Males will go on organized hunting expeditions. They will hunt and kill monkeys, baboons, pigs, and even small antelope. A group of animals works together to ambush or chase prey. Chases can be very noisy and last up to two hours. When a victim is caught, the chimps go into a frenzy of excitement and tear it apart.

Tool Users

The use of tools to help perform additional tasks that cannot be completed with bare hands used to be considered one of the key differences between humans and all other species of animals. However, it is now known that several nonhuman species often use tools—chimpanzees foremost among them. Chimps show a great deal of intelligence in their choice, preparation, and use of tools. They strip leaves off long, thin sticks to poke around in termite nests, and use bent sticks to pull down fruit-laden branches that are otherwise out of reach. Sticks are also used as weapons, levers, and even to clean teeth. They use leaves to wipe themselves clean or to pick up sticky food. Leaves are also used to collect drinking water from tree holes. Spongy leaves are chewed first to make them more absorbent. Some chimps use stones to crack open hard nuts. They use a "hammer and anvil" technique, choosing a rock or exposed tree root as an anvil and a large, carefully selected stone as a hammer. Hammer stones can weigh up to 20 pounds (9 kg) and need to be held at just the right angle and used with enough force to crack the nut without spoiling the edible kernel

⊕ *A chimpanzee in Liberia cracks a nut with a stone, using a tree trunk as an anvil. Chimps show a great deal of intelligence in their use of objects, such as sticks and stones, as both tools and weapons.*

Chimp Culture

Chimps show cultural traditions that are learned and passed on in the group. One example is in tool use. Some chimpanzee communities use stones as hammers to crack nuts, while other groups have never learned the trick. In one part of Africa chimps crack oil palm nuts. Another community farther away uses heavier stones to break open harder nuts, and the animals ignore the easier oil palms. Yet another group of chimpanzees uses branches as wooden clubs, but few others are known to do so.

inside. Good hammer stones are hard to find in the forest, so chimps use the same one time and time again, remembering where they left it and carrying it from one place to another.

Playful as a Chimp

Young chimpanzees are born very small and helpless. The mother carries her baby under her belly until it is old enough to hang onto her chest hair. After five or six months the baby rides sitting upright on its mother's back.

Young chimps are extremely curious and playful. They will examine anything they can reach, including any other chimps that the mother will allow near. Other chimps are always very curious about new babies. They have to earn the right to come close to the baby, usually by giving the mother grooming sessions.

Weaning begins when the baby is at least three years old. The young chimp learns which foods are good to eat by exploring everything its mother has, often chewing the other end of whatever she eats. Mothers encourage their young to eat certain plants by dropping them in their path and discourage them from poisonous ones by taking them out of their hands.

Young chimps are taught by their mother, but also learn by experimentation or through watching others. Learning how to groom, recognizing group members, and learning the rules of social behavior are vital if a chimp is to get on in a community. Many lessons are learned during play: Hours are spent in rough-and-tumble and play-fighting games.

By the age of five a young chimp may be physically independent of its mother, but still very close to her emotionally. As they get older, juvenile chimps spend less time with their mother, and males increasingly venture out with gangs of other young males. Many females, however, stay with their mothers for the rest of their lives. However, some young females leave their birth group and join another. It is a risky venture, and it may be many years before they are fully integrated into the new community.

A female chimpanzee is receptive for 10 of the 36 days of her estrus cycle and advertises the fact with a pink swelling at her rear. During that time she is irresistible to males and may mate often. The top male in the group tries to monopolize mating opportunities by keeping close by, grooming her, and fending off other males. A lower-ranking male may be able to gain her favor, but has to attract her attention without the rest of the group noticing. Sometimes these illicit couples leave the group and disappear into the forest together for the duration of her fertile phase or even longer. The male then has a guarantee of being the father of the offspring, but both animals risk finding it difficult to rejoin the group or losing their rank in the social hierarchy.

Threats to Survival

Huge areas of African forests have been cut down for timber or to grow cash crops. What is left is very fragmented, with small pockets of trees that can only support a few isolated animals. Chimps are also killed to supply the bushmeat trade and were captured for zoos, the entertainment industry, and for biomedical research. The only way to catch a live baby chimp is to kill its mother, and many other members of the group may be killed or injured in the process.

Chimps in the Rain

Chimpanzees detest the rain, since their fur is not waterproof. They are normally up at dawn, but are reluctant to get out of bed if it is raining and shelter under trees or sit hunched up waiting for it to stop. However, a rainstorm sometimes encourages a male to perform a bizarre rain dance. First he rocks gently, then he stamps his feet, waves his arms, and throws branches around as though he is having a temper tantrum at the weather.

➔ *A juvenile chimp plays with an adult. Young chimps are extremely curious about their new environment, but adults are also interested in new additions to the group.*

Common name
Bonobo (pygmy chimpanzee)

Scientific name *Pan paniscus*

Family Hominidae

Order Primates

Size Length head/body: 27.5–33 in (70–83 cm)

Weight Male up to 88 lb (40 kg); female up to 68 lb (31 kg)

Key features Looks like a long-legged chimpanzee, but body more slender with narrower shoulders; skin of face dark brown to black

Habits Active during the day in trees and on the ground; sleeps in nests built among tree branches; social groups more female centered, with the most dominant female ranking above the dominant male

Breeding Single young born at any time of year after gestation period of 220–230 days. Weaned at 4 years; females sexually mature at 9 years, males earlier, although both unlikely to breed until older. May live to possibly 30 years in the wild, rarely kept in captivity

Voice Calls more high pitched than chimpanzee

Diet Fruit, leaves, stems, shoots, and honey; also termites, ants, and small reptiles

Habitat Tropical lowland rain forest

Distribution Restricted to northern-central Democratic Republic of Congo south of Congo River and between the Kasai and Sankuru Rivers

Status Population: about 15,000; IUCN Endangered; CITES I. Habitat loss and hunting have contributed to decline

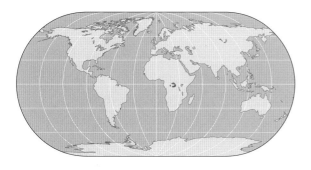

Bonobo

Pan paniscus

Genetic analysis of the bonobo suggests that it may be even more closely related to humans than its better-known cousin the chimpanzee.

THE BONOBO, OR PYGMY CHIMPANZEE, was not recognized as a separate species from the common chimpanzee until the 1920s. Nobody is certain how the species came to be known as the bonobo, but it is thought that perhaps the name may have arisen from a mispronunciation of the town of Bolobo in the Democratic Republic of Congo (DRC). It was there that scientists first came across the animals. Bonobos live in the dense rain forests of the Congo River Basin of central DRC in Africa.

Slender Build
Although bonobos are often referred to as "pygmy chimpanzees," they are not actually very different in size from their chimp cousins. The main physical difference is that bonobos have a lighter build and relatively longer limbs. Other differences are that bonobos generally have narrower shoulders, a thinner neck, and a smaller, rounder head than the common chimpanzee. Bonobo distribution does not overlap with that of the common chimpanzee. Also, despite the behavior and lifestyle of the two species being similar in some ways, bonobo society is generally more relaxed and friendly.

Like humans and all living apes, bonobos have no tail. Studies of the chromosomes of primates reveal striking similarities between apes and humans, with the bonobo being more similar to us than any other animal.

Bonobos have a distinctive flattened shock of hair on the head that often parts down the middle. Juveniles and adults may have a white patch of fur on the lower part of their back, and babies are born with a black face. An adult male weighs about 88 pounds (40 kg); a female is about one-third smaller. Males also tend to have larger, more prominent canine teeth.

⬆ *The bonobo looks rather like a more slender, long-legged version of its cousin the chimpanzee. Yet it was not recognized as a species separate from the common chimpanzee until the 1920s.*

trees, bonobos are more acrobatic than common chimpanzees, often jumping from branch to branch.

Sexual Bonding

Groups of bonobos range from about 50 to 200 individuals. The groups will break up during the day, forming smaller parties of between six and 15 that forage for food together. The groups are generally larger than the foraging groups of the common chimpanzee. Perhaps that is why the bonobo is more sociable and less aggressive than other chimpanzees. Sexual acts are used as a way of reinforcing friendships and as a greeting between all members of the group. Even among primates such a high level of sexual interaction is unique to bonobos. It seems to reduce tension between group members and is thought to be one of the reasons why bonobos are so rarely aggressive toward each other.

The bonobo is now considered a threatened species. Habitat destruction, hunting, and collection for the illegal pet trade have led to a drastic decline in bonobo numbers. The problem is worsened by the fact that a single female will have relatively few young in her lifetime. It may be 12 or 13 years before a female gives birth to her first infant. The baby will take about four to five years to rear, and even after five years a juvenile bonobo may remain emotionally dependent on its mother. Consequently, bonobo populations grow very slowly and cannot easily compensate for large numbers of animals killed by hunters or captured as pets. A bonobo protection fund was founded in 1990 to help bonobo conservation and teach the people of the DRC about the importance of wildlife preservation.

Bonobos survive mostly on fruit, but during the dry season when fruit is scarce, plant shoots, leaves, and flowers are also eaten. It has been estimated that the animals may use over 100 different plant species in the course of a year. Their diet may also include termites, worms, small reptiles, and even flying squirrels.

The bonobo is diurnal. Each night the animals will retire into the treetops and construct a new nest from branches and leaves, where they spend the hours of darkness. They actually spend more time in the trees than common chimpanzees, but they are also often active at ground level. When they are up in the

The Gibbon Family

The gibbons, or lesser apes, are a distinctive group of primates. With their extremely long arms and legs they hang and swing through the trees searching for fruit. They are one of the few primates that are completely monogamous, with males and females often staying together for life. Each pair defends a territory, using loud, distinctive calls that in Southeast Asia are the most characteristic sounds of the rain forest.

Gibbons live in the evergreen rain forests and semideciduous monsoon forests of Asia. They occur from the eastern edge of India to the far south of China and through Bangladesh, Sumatra, and western Java and Borneo. There are no gibbons in Africa or the Americas. There are 11 species, all in the same genus (*Hylobates*). The different species of gibbon can be told apart by their coat color and markings, their calls, and the areas where they live: Very few species have overlapping distributions.

What Is a Gibbon?

Gibbons are slender, graceful animals with long limbs. Like the apes, they have no tail. Males and females are the same size, unlike some of the apes, in which males tend to be larger. The coat color varies widely between species, particularly around the head and face, and sometimes between the sexes. Some species have throat pouches that are used to enhance the resonance of their calls. Gibbons move through the trees by swinging from the branches, grasping them with their long, slender fingers and hurling themselves from one support to the next. They also frequently walk upright, both on the ground and also running along horizontal branches, demonstrating a great sense of balance. However, their arms are so long that they get in the way when running on two legs. Therefore, gibbons much prefer to hang from branches rather than stand up.

Their diet consists mainly of fruit and leaves, with some insects and other invertebrates. They prefer ripe, pulpy fruit and often perform an important role in dispersing tree seeds in their dung. Many seeds are more likely to germinate after they have passed through the gibbon's digestive system, which weakens the seed coat. They are deposited some distance away from the parent tree with a ready supply of fertilizer.

Gibbon Songs

Gibbons' songs are loud and complex, with a purity and melancholy unmatched in any primate other than humans. Before sunrise males start to call while still in the nest. The call starts as a soft warbling and develops over the half hour or so until sunrise into a loud and elaborate song. The females sing later in the morning, in shorter, simpler, but highly impressive sessions. They call from the treetops, making a great display of swinging between trees, breaking branches, and crashing them to the floor. The same song is repeated over and over again in a crescendo, ending in a lively climax. In many species males accompany the females in duets. Their calls appear to be primarily territorial signals. While females seem to sing to defend the territory, males apparently sing to defend the females from other males. By singing in duets, they may be advertising that they have a stable pair bond, and that attention from others is unwelcome.

Lifestyle

Gibbons are monogamous, meaning that they stay with a single partner, often for life. A pair will defend a territory that varies in size depending on the habitat. On average an area of forest that covers 0.4 square miles (1 sq. km) will support between two and four family groups. The

---

Family Hylobatidae: 1 genus, 11 species

Hylobates, including lar gibbon (*H. lar*); siamang (*H. syndactylus*); kloss gibbon (*H. klossii*); moloch gibbon (*H. moloch*); Müller's gibbon (*H. muelleri*); crested black gibbon (*H. concolor*)

A Müller's gibbon swinging through the forests of Kalimantan, Borneo. Gibbon habitat is decreasing rapidly, owing to logging and agricultural practices.

A female kloss gibbon announces her territory by calling loudly while in midair (1). She may also run upright along branches, tearing off leaves (2).

territories are announced by calls from the center, usually by the female. Calls from the boundary reinforce the border if other gibbons venture too close. If that does not deter intruders, confrontations are followed by a chase. Rarely does it end in physical clashes.

Young are born after a gestation period of seven to eight months, and sexual maturity is reached after a period of about six years. The females become pregnant every two or three years, so the family group usually consists of two to four immature offspring and their parents. Unless there is a particularly large food source, gibbons tend to forage alone up to 165 feet (50 m) away from each other. They will come together for rest, grooming, and sometimes sleeping. Siamangs maintain much closer links when foraging, usually being less than 100 feet (30 m) away. Grooming is important in maintaining bonds, and adults will groom each other, their subadults, and the young. They also spend time in play, centered on the youngest infant.

One of the most serious threats to the survival of all the gibbon species is logging. The rapid destruction of forests in Southeast Asia has brought the kloss, moloch, and some crested gibbons to the edge of extinction, and is seriously threatening the survival of other species too.

Common name Lar gibbon (common gibbon, white-handed gibbon)

Scientific name *Hylobates lar*

Family Hylobatidae

Order Primates

Size Length head/body: 18–25 in (45–64 cm)

Weight 12–14 lb (5–6 kg)

Key features Coat color varies between populations—either black, dark brown, reddish brown, or light buff; long, spindly limbs with pale hands and feet; no tail; pale ring around face

Habits Lives high in rainforest trees, swinging between branches; active by day; family groups are territorial, announcing their presence with loud calls

Breeding Single infant born about every 2 years after gestation period of 7–8 months. Weaned at 20 months; sexually mature at 6–7 years. May live up to about 40 years in captivity, 30–40 in the wild

Voice Male's song is simple hoots, female's longer, rising to a climax

Diet Mainly fruit; also leaves, birds, and insects

Habitat Evergreen rain forest; semideciduous monsoon forest

Distribution Thailand, Malay Peninsula, and northern Sumatra

Status Population: about 79,000 (1987); IUCN Endangered; CITES I

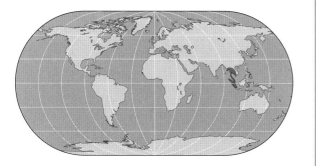

Lar Gibbon

Hylobates lar

Lar gibbons are the most active of all the gibbons. Using their long arms to swing through the trees, they travel high among the branches looking for their favorite food of figs.

THE LAR, OR COMMON, GIBBON is the best known of all 11 gibbon species and is the one most often seen in zoos. Its coat color is variable, depending on where the animal lives, but males and females within the same population always look similar. In Malaysia they are dark brown to buff, in Sumatra they are reddish-brown or buff, and in Thailand they are either black or pale cream. They have a white ring of fur around the face and pale hands and feet—hence their other name of white-handed gibbon.

Life in the Trees

Gibbons live high in the middle and upper layers of the rain forest. They spend almost their whole time 100 feet (30 m) high in the trees, rarely coming to the ground. Because the forests are so dense, very little grows in the dark lower levels, so the gibbons have no particular reason to descend. Moreover, their long limbs make walking around on the ground rather difficult, so they are vulnerable to predators once they have left the safety of the treetops. Their bodies are perfectly adapted to life spent high in the branches, and lar gibbons move faster and farther each day than any other forest ape or monkey.

All gibbons have a small, athletic body, with very long arms, long fingers that are good for grasping, and relatively small thumbs. Their usual way of getting around is by swinging hand over hand from branches and creepers (known as brachiation). They are incredibly agile and precise in their movements. They possess remarkable hand–eye coordination and split-second timing. They can easily leap 30 feet (9 m) between trees; and if the branch that they are swinging from breaks, they can make a mid-

air twist to grab a branch lower down. They are quick enough to be able to catch birds and insects that fly past.

Gibbons feed hanging from their arms or even an arm and a leg, collecting fruit from the ends of branches. They usually choose ripe fruits, picking them carefully by hand, and leaving unripe ones. About 75 percent of their diet is ripe fruit, with figs being a particular favorite. They also eat leaves, young shoots, flowers, birds' eggs, insects, and spiders that they find among the forest canopy.

Gibbons spend most of the day foraging. They may visit 16 or more widely spaced fruit trees in a day. Rather than coming down to a puddle or stream, they drink by licking their body after a rainstorm. Otherwise, they will dip an arm into a tree hole or rub it on wet leaves, then lick the resulting moisture from their fur.

At the end of the day they sleep, squatting on the branch of a tall tree. Like baboons, gibbons have ischial callosities (bare "sitting patches") on their rump to protect them from the rough bark. They like to sleep in a tree that is higher than the others in the forest, since it

⊕ A female lar gibbon with an infant. Lar gibbons have a long weaning period, which is not completed until the offspring is about 20 months old. Gibbons are venerated as spirits by the indigenous forest peoples of Indonesia and the Malay Peninsula, who tend not to hunt them.

will give them a good singing position for their morning calls.

Territorial Singing

Lar gibbons, like all other gibbons, are highly territorial. Each pair defends a home range of about 37 acres (15 ha). In areas where there are fewer gibbons, or the habitat quality is lower, territories can be as large as 124 acres (50 ha). They warn other gibbons off their patch by singing, usually for about half an hour every morning. The males and females "duet," singing together with different calls. The male has a shrill "quaver song," while the female has a plaintive swooping call, rising to a crescendo. The calls can be heard up to 2 miles (3 km) away. Occasionally, rival groups meet, which may result in a fight, usually between males.

Lar gibbons choose a mate for life. The pair produce a baby every two years or so. Infants stay with their parents for about six years, so there are likely to be two or three young of different ages in the family. When a baby is about a year old, the father takes over its care, only returning it to its mother to be breast-fed.

The Old World Monkey Family

All African primates, with the exception of the great apes and the nocturnal bush babies and their relatives, belong to the family Cercopithecidae. Members of this family also occur in Asia and in Gibraltar (at the southern tip of Spain, where they may have been introduced).

The Old World monkeys are what most people class as "real monkeys" and are familiar because many species are kept in zoos. In the wild they often come into contact with humans, since they raid crops or feed near or in villages. Some are hunted for their meat and fur or captured for use in laboratory research.

What Are Old World Monkeys?

Most members of the family are tree-living. Macaques, however, are equally at home on the ground or in trees, and baboons spend most of their time on the ground. Old World monkeys can stand upright, but generally move around on four limbs. Most are good swimmers. Nearly all are active during the day, not at night, and have good eyesight, hearing, and sense of smell.

There are two main groups of Old World monkeys: the colobus and leaf monkeys, or colobines, and the cercopithecines—the guenons, mangabeys, macaques, and baboons. Colobines are slender, have long limbs, large bodies, small heads, and almost no thumb. They are also known as thumbless monkeys. Because they specialize in eating leaves, they have large salivary glands and an unusual chambered stomach. Cercopithecines are more diverse, ranging from the miniature talapoin monkey and the colorful guenon monkeys to the stocky, large-headed baboons. They are sometimes also called cheek-pouch monkeys.

Colobus and Leaf Monkeys

Colobus and leaf monkeys (colobines) are long-tailed monkeys that spend most of their time in the trees. Almost all of them eat leaves.

Family Cercopithecidae: 2 subfamilies, 18 genera, 91 species

Subfamily Cercopithecinae (baboons and typical monkeys) 11 genera, 49 species

Cercocebus 2 species, agile mangabey (*C. galeritus*); white mangabey (*C. torquatus*)

Lophocebus 2 species, gray-cheeked mangabey (*L. albigena*); black mangabey (*L. aterrimus*)

Cercopithecus 18 species, including mustached monkey (*C. cephus*); De Brazza's monkey (*C. neglectus*)

Chlorocebus 1 species, vervet monkey (*C. aethiops*)

Allenopithecus 1 species, Allen's swamp monkey (*A. nigroviridis*)

Miopithecus 1 species, talapoin monkey (*M. talapoin*)

Erythrocebus 1 species, patas monkey (*E. patas*)

Macaca 15 species, including Japanese macaque (*M. fuscata*); Barbary macaque (*M. sylvanus*); black macaque (*M. nigra*); lion-tailed macaque (*M. silenus*)

Papio 5 species, including savanna baboon (*P. cynocephalus*); hamadryas baboon (*P. hamadryas*)

Mandrillus 2 species, drill (*M. leucophaeus*); mandrill (*M. sphinx*)

Theropithecus 1 species, gelada (*T. gelada*)

Subfamily Colobinae (leaf monkeys) 7 genera, 42 species

Nasalis 2 species, proboscis monkey (*N. larvatus*); simakobu (*N. (Simias) concolor*)

Pygathrix 6 species, including golden snub-nosed monkey (*P. (Rhinopithecus) roxellana*)

Presbytis 8 species, including grizzled sureli (*P. comata*); banded sureli (*P. femoralis*)

Semnopithecus 2 species, Hanuman langur (*S. entellus*); Malabar langur (*S. hypoleucos*)

Trachypithecus 13 species, including dusky leaf monkey (*T. (Semnopithecus) obscurus*); golden leaf monkey (*T. (S.) geei*)

Colobus 5 species, including satanic black colobus (*C. satanus*); black-and-white colobus (*C. angolensis*)

Procolobus 6 species, including western red colobus (*P. badius*)

1

 SEE ALSO Ape Family, The **4**:12; Bush Baby, Demidoff's **4**:110

→ *A lion-tailed macaque vocalizing. Lion-tailed macaques inhabit the wet forests of southern India, where they live most of their lives in the trees and very rarely come to the ground.*

Cellulose is the main component of leaves, and mammals cannot deal with it easily. The leaves also sometimes contain toxins. To aid digestion, colobines have a partitioned stomach. In the first chamber fermenting bacteria break down the tough cellulose into sugar; they can also break down poisons. The Hanuman langur is able to eat fruits containing the poison strychnine, which would be fatal to other primates. Because leaves are not very nutritious, monkeys have to eat a lot, and the stomach contents can make up a quarter of an adult's body weight. Another feature is that the thumbs are reduced to stumps. That is particularly marked in colobus monkeys (colobus means "docked" in Greek).

Asian Stronghold

There are over 40 species of leaf monkey, forming seven genera. Their stronghold is Asia, with 31 species from five genera,

compared with 11 species from two genera in Africa. Borneo is home to six species of colobine, including the bizarre-looking proboscis monkey and a couple of surelis. Their genus name, *Presbytis*, means "old woman" and refers to their wrinkled and wizened faces. The red colobus monkeys, members of the *Procolobus* genus, live in the rain forests and savanna of equatorial Africa. Their

← *Small and medium-sized cercopithecines: gray-cheeked mangabey (western race with double crest) (1); Allen's swamp monkey (2); mustached monkey (3); talapoin, the smallest Old World monkey (4); patas monkey (5).*

3

4

2

5

coats are multicolored and vary from region to region. The paws, back, and tail tip are often blackish-red; the brow may be white or orange, and the cheeks and chest are orange or yellowish-white. Black colobus monkeys found in western, central, and eastern Africa are various shades of black and white or gray. The leaf monkeys and langurs all have ridges on their faces that make them look as if they are raising their eyebrows.

Colobines are often described as "solemn." They use few gestures and calls and have low levels of aggression. That is likely to be because their food is widely dispersed, so there is less need for troop coordination.

"Cheek-Pouch Monkeys" (cercopithecines)

The mangabeys, macaques, guenons, and baboons are known as the cheek-pouch monkeys because they often fill their cheeks with food for transportation. They are sociable, noisy, and curious animals. These cercopithecines are also well known because their distribution and habits (some unpopular, such as raiding crops) often bring them into contact with people.

Apart from the guenons, most cercopithecines have a fairly long muzzle, with baboons being the most extreme examples. In baboons, mangabeys, and macaques there are brightly colored patches of bare skin on the face and rump (and in the gelada on the chest too). In female baboons, mangabeys, some macaques, and some guenons the skin around their genitals swells and

becomes brightly colored. The colored swellings signal readiness to mate or, in some species, that they are pregnant.

There are over 40 species of cercopithecine in seven genera. The drill and mandrill live on the forest floor of western-central Africa. The mandrill is the largest of the baboons. Both species are mainly black with a short tail.

Guenons have distinctive coat colors that vary between species. Most stay in trees, except the patas monkey, whose long legs make it the fastest runner of all the primates. It can reach speeds of up to 34 miles per hour (55 km/h).

The most widespread guenon is the vervet monkey. It is always found close to water and spends much of its time in acacia trees along riverbanks.

Mangabeys are sometimes called long-tailed baboons. All live in thick canopy forests. Gray-cheeked and black mangabeys spend most of their time in the treetops, while the agile and white mangabeys prefer to stay on the ground, like baboons.

Macaques are at home on the ground or in trees. The Barbary macaque is a hardy mountain dweller that lives in northern Algeria, Morocco, and Gibraltar. Other macaques live in Asia. The Japanese macaque has a shaggy coat that keeps it warm in the snowy winters of northern Japan. Rhesus monkeys and other macaques will often raid fields in India.

Baboons are the largest of the monkeys. They are found almost everywhere in Africa and are mainly ground-living. The savanna baboon lives in grasslands and

Demanding Females

Unusually for animals, it is the females of most colobines that encourage the mating process. A receptive female proboscis monkey will eye a male, pursing her lips. If he returns her glance, she shakes her head (which means "yes," not "no.") The male responds by pouting and either approaches her, or she will approach him, presenting her rear. In Hanuman langurs, if the male ignores a female's suggestive glances, she will hit him, pull his fur, and even bite him.

⊙ *De Brazza's monkey, one of the colorful cercopithecine species, has a distinctive white beard and an orange "diadem" on its brow. Like most other cercopithecines, it lives in groups and is semiterrestrial.*

large molar teeth for grinding. Geladas, which live almost solely on grass, also have large molars. They pick it with their hands, using each hand alternately.

Other species are mainly fruit feeders, but all of them will eat anything edible that they come across, including seeds, flowers, buds, leaves, bark, gum, roots, bulbs, insects, snails, crabs, fish, lizards, birds, and mammals. Savanna baboons will eat mollusks, and talapoins are said to dive for fish. Most species are fairly experimental with food and will learn from each other ways of preparing food and what is good to eat. When feeding in an exposed area, the monkeys will stuff their cheek pouches with as much food as possible, then retire to a safer place to chew at leisure. The talapoin is the smallest of the Old World monkeys and lives in the flood-plain forests of western-central Africa.

Troop Life

Cercopithecines are more sociable than their relatives the colobines. Most live in noisy troops, using frequent calls, gestures, and aggression to interact with each other. The two main types of group are single male and multimale. Baboons, mangabeys, and macaques tend to live in large, multimale troops. In hamadryas baboons and geladas such troops may be made up of smaller subgroups, each with a single male. Males living together in a troop establish hierarchies through aggressive competitive behavior. The ranks are changeable, so there are frequent spats as animals test each other's dominance. Patas monkeys and most forest guenons have single-male troops. Adult males that do not belong to troops are usually found alone, although sometimes they band together in small temporary groups.

Cercopithecines are slow to mature and reproduce, but they live a long time. The fastest maturing is the patas monkey, which can breed at about two and a half years old. In contrast, the talapoin takes the longest time to mature, not breeding until it is four or five years old.

bush. Others can be found in lowlands, rain forest, and in desert regions. Baboons have naked faces and a long muzzle, rather like a dog. Males and females often look very different from each other. In hamadryas baboons, for example, the male has long silvery gray hair and a bright-red face and rump. However, the female's coat is brown, and she has a dark-colored face.

Baboons eat a lot of grass and during the dry season dig up bulbs and other succulent plant parts. They have

Common name Vervet monkey (savanna guenon, grivet, or green monkey)

Scientific name *Cercopithecus aethiops*

Family Cercopithecidae

Order Primates

Size Length head/body: male 20–26 in (50–65 cm); female 15–24 in (38–62 cm); tail length: 19–30 in (48–75 cm)

Weight Male 9–18 lb (4–8 kg); female 8–11 lb (4–5 kg)

Key features Back and outer limbs grizzled gray or olive, underparts white; dark hands, feet, and tip of tail; face is bare and black, with white cheek tufts and eyebrows; eyelids white; scrotum bright blue, penis red

Habits Alert, lively, sociable monkey; active during the day; spends time on the ground as well as in trees

Breeding Single young usually born in favorable season after gestation period of 7 months. Weaned at 8–9 months; females sexually mature at 2 years, males at 3 years. May live up to about 30 years in captivity, 10 in the wild

Voice Includes barks, grunts, and screams

Diet Mainly fruit; also leaves, flowers, and crops; occasionally insects, eggs, nestlings, and small animals

Habitat Savanna and woodland edges near water

Distribution Most of Africa: Senegal east to Somalia and south to South Africa

Status Population: abundant, many thousands. Common and widespread

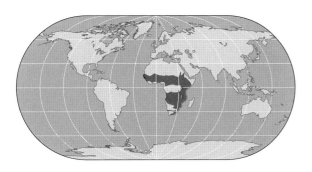

Vervet Monkey

Cercopithecus aethiops

Vervets are successful, adaptable monkeys, living throughout a large part of Africa in many different habitats. They thrive almost anywhere where there is water and fruiting trees.

THE VERVET IS ONE OF THE GUENONS, a group of small- to medium-sized monkeys that have a long tail, grizzled fur, and dramatic face patterns. All guenons live in Africa. Vervets are the most widespread of the group, living across a large swath of the continent north and south of the equator and at altitudes of up to 10,000 feet (3,000 m). There are around 16 local variants throughout Africa, each differing slightly in appearance, but able to interbreed where their regions overlap.

Striking Looks

Vervets have a striking appearance, with their black face framed by white eyebrows and long, white cheek fur. The males have a turquoise blue scrotum and a red penis. The back, crown, and outer limbs are grizzled, gray, olive, or brownish, depending on the region in which the animal lives. In the eastern parts of southern Africa they are gray, becoming more olive green in the west. From the Indian Ocean to the great lakes of the Rift Valley they are an olive-fawn color; on the Atlantic side of Africa they are olive-gray with a blotched face; and in Somalia they are brownish. The underside is white; the hands and feet are dark. The long tail has a dark tip and red tufts at its base, but it cannot be used for gripping branches, as in many American monkeys.

Unlike other guenons, which tend to be forest dwelling, vervets prefer more open areas. They live mainly on the savanna and in lightly

wooded areas. Their favorite habitat is in the acacia trees that line riverbanks, but they are very flexible about the types of habitat that they occupy. They are also found along the edges of rain forest, in mangrove swamps, and even on agricultural land. In fact, they seem able to live anywhere there is water and enough trees to supply fruit, shade, and somewhere to sleep.

The vervet monkey's diet consists mainly of fruit, particularly figs. Outside the fruiting season, when such food is not available, they will eat flowers, buds, and leaves. Acacia trees are also an important source of food, providing seeds, flowers, fruit, and gum. Vervets often raid crops and can become a pest in coffee plantations. They will also eat some animal food, such as invertebrates, especially insects, eggs, and small lizards and mice. However, their tiny thumbs mean that they are not very good at catching and handling live insects or other small, active sorts of prey.

When foraging for food, vervets are equally happy on the ground as in the trees. However, they may spend a lot of time out of the trees, particularly when there is no fruit available. But they will always try to keep close enough to trees to allow a swift escape off the ground if danger threatens. Vervets always sleep in trees. They are good climbers, but only rarely leap from tree to tree. They come down from the trees head first. When on the ground, they walk or use a fast, bounding gallop on all four limbs. In tall grass they will run on their hind legs to get a better view. They can also swim, but do so only occasionally.

Inherited Rank

Vervets are sociable animals. They live in groups (called troops) of about two dozen animals, but sometimes as many as 70 or as few as five. Troops usually include several males, and both

⊖ *Vervet monkeys look very striking. Their black faces are framed by white eyebrows and white cheek fur. Their body fur can be a gray, fawn, or olive shade.*

the males and females adopt a hierarchy of dominance. High-ranking individuals have priority when there is competition for food, and high-ranking males also perform most of the matings. Rank within females is inherited, so a daughter born to a high-ranking mother automatically has a high rank herself. Rank also depends on age. If more than one female in the group is ready to breed, the males will tend to prefer the older one. Similarly, females tend to prefer older males. The males are usually dominant over the females, but females will often band together to prevent males from attacking their young.

Although a troop will forage and sleep close together, the animals tend to interact mainly with close family members. Such practices are especially common among females. Individuals within a family form close bonds and will sit together and groom each other. They will also defend each other in fights. Juveniles tend to form close bonds among themselves, and young males will carry and care for younger relatives. However, adult males show no interest in infants. Mothers will allow other females to hold their babies, and the young of high-ranking females seem to be preferred for such "fondling."

Daughters stay with their mothers in the same social group as long as they live, while sons usually leave the troop when they become sexually mature. They will go to join a neighboring troop, losing their inherited rank.

Vervets are alert monkeys. High-ranking males are especially cautious and are constantly looking out for trouble, whether in the form of a predator or a gang of rival males. Vervets are at risk from many predators, including eagles, leopards, and pythons, which often wait in ambush at the base of trees.

Troop Signals

Living in a group demands a certain amount of coordination and communication. Vervets have a wide range of calls that they use to communicate warnings, threats, submission, or pleas for help. When defending territories, they will use a loud bark. Both males and females use a "chutter" of low staccato barks as an aggressive threat and to call for support from the rest of the group. If two vervets within the troop are fighting, others will use a low bark to encourage them to stop. A deep, guttural "woof" or exhaled "wa" sound shows submission by a lower-ranking male to a more dominant animal. Females and juveniles let out a high-pitched, piercing scream or squeal if they feel threatened and want assistance. Members of the troop give a nasal grunt when they are about to move off to a new area.

Vervets have a complex system of alarm calls, with different calls for different predators. For example, they give a short, sharp "chirp" call for mammalian predators, such as leopards, and a short, rough "rraup" for birds of prey. The different calls allow the others in the troop to take appropriate action. On a "leopard" call the group runs into the trees. On an alarm call for an "eagle" the animals look up and run into the bushes, while a "snake" alarm call causes them to stand up on their hind legs and peer into the grass around them.

As well as their extensive range of calls, vervets also use visual and tactile signals to communicate. When a vervet is standing on all fours, the position of the tail is a good clue to the animal's mood. When feeling confident, a vervet holds his tail high, arched over the body.

Defending Territory with Red, White, and Blue

Vervets are highly territorial and will defend their home range against other troops. Although females are territorial, the males are most active in defense of their home area. When two troops meet, they use aggressive calls and body language to intimidate their rivals. The males use a threat display known as "red, white, and blue" in which they walk back and forth or stand upright, each displaying its bright-red penis and blue scrotum to the intruders.

⬆ *A troop of vervet monkeys perches in the lower branches of a tree in the Moremi Reserve, Botswana. Troops can number anything from five to 70 individuals. Dominance hierarchies operate within the troop, with rank being inherited from parents.*

 SEE ALSO Leopard 2:30

If fearful, the animal will hold his tail lower, parallel to the ground. Staring with raised eyebrows and head bobbing are both threat displays, while rapid glancing toward and away from an aggressor indicates submission. When two vervets meet, they touch muzzles together in a nose-to-nose greeting. It is usually followed by play or grooming, which is an important way of maintaining social bonds.

Flexible Breeding

One of the reasons for the vervets' success is their flexible breeding rate. Females can breed at any time of year, but numbers of births tend to peak during the seasons when food is most abundant. During times of drought or famine they are less likely to reproduce; but when good times return, they quickly resume breeding.

When a female is receptive, she will present herself to the male to encourage mating. A single infant is subsequently born, although occasionally there are twins. A mother will nurse her young until the next infant is born, which will usually be the following year.

Young vervet monkeys mature quickly: Females are able to reproduce in two years and males in three. However, females do not reach full adult size until they are four years old, and males take five years to reach maturity.

⊕ *Two vervets in the Kruger National Park, South Africa, take turns in mutual grooming. As in other primates, grooming is an important way of maintaining social bonds.*

Common name Japanese macaque (snow monkey)

Scientific name *Macaca fuscata*

Family Cercopithecidae

Order Primates

Size Length head/body: 18.5–24 in (47–60 cm); tail length: 3–5 in (7–12 cm)

Weight Male 22–40 lb (10–18 kg); female 15.5–26.5 lb (7–12 kg)

Key features Thick, brown to gray coat; bare, red-colored face and buttocks; short tail

Habits Active by day; highly social: lives in troops averaging 20–30 animals, but sometimes up to 100; forages on ground and in trees

Breeding Single infant born every 2 years (usually between May and September) after gestation period of 5–6 months. Weaned at 6 months; females sexually mature at 3–4 years, but usually first breed at 6, males sexually mature at 5–6 years. May live up to about 30 years in captivity, similar in the wild

Voice Various long- and short-distance calls

Diet Fruit, insects, young leaves, and small animals; sometimes raids crops

Habitat Upland and mountain broad-leaved forest

Distribution Japan

Status Population: about 35,000–50,000 (1990); IUCN previously Endangered, temporarily listed as Data Deficient (2000); CITES II. Listed as Threatened by U.S. Endangered Species Act, but status in wild disputed

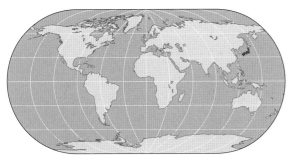

Japanese Macaque

Macaca fuscata

Also known as the snow monkey, the Japanese macaque frequents the cold mountains of Japan. It lives in large groups with strict hierarchies, often with close bonds between individuals.

JAPANESE MACAQUES ARE medium-sized monkeys with gray to brown fur, which is very dense, especially in winter. The bare face is bright red in adults. They also have red skin on their buttocks. The tail is short and stumpy.

Japanese macaques live in the forests of the highlands and mountains of Japan. Their thick fur helps them survive in the cold, snowy winters. Japanese macaques are the only nonhuman primates living in Japan, and they occur farther north than any other primate. In northern parts of their range temperatures can vary between 5°F (–15°C) in winter and 73°F (23°C) in summer. To cope, the macaques molt so that in summer they have a thin coat, while for winter the fur grows long and dense.

In some parts of Japan the macaques survive the worst of the weather by spending time in warm baths formed by hot springs. The whole troop will sit calmly together, relaxing in the warm water while snow falls around them. Many groups of macaques have also been seen making snowballs in the same way that human children do. It appears to be a social pastime, in which the whole troop can be involved.

Seasonal Diet

Japanese macaques are primarily vegetarian. Most of their food consists of fruit, plus seeds, leaves, flowers, and buds. They also eat crops such as rice and corn. They may sometimes supplement their diet with insects and other invertebrates, together with occasional birds' eggs and small mammals. In the northern parts of their range much of the food is only available seasonally. During the fall there are plenty of

fruits and berries, but in spring, the animals have to eat more young leaves and flowers. In winter they must resort to tree bark and buds. During the winter the macaques rely on stored body fat, since what is available to eat may be less than half their daily nutritional needs. In more southern parts, where the seasons are less extreme, some fruit is available all year round.

Japanese macaques live in large groups called troops. Social order is strictly maintained within the troop. Both males and females have hierarchies. At the top there is a dominant, or alpha male. Below him are male subleaders. The females come third in rank, followed by the nonleaders and other juvenile animals. When traveling, the macaques line up according to rank, with the subleaders at the front, the dominant males behind them guarding the females and their babies, and other subleaders and juveniles following at the rear.

In males hierarchy is determined by size and strength; in females it is inherited. Females stay within the group into which they were born, but males leave when they are sexually mature. Females prefer to mate with different males each season, so long-standing males have less chance of mating if they stay in that troop.

Experimenting with Food

Different troops have different habits, mostly relating to types of food eaten. Preferences are passed through the troop by imitation. It is often the young macaques that discover new things, since they are more inquisitive. In one troop researchers dropped grains of wheat on a beach. One young female discovered that she could scoop them up and wash them in the sea. The sand would sink, making it easy to collect the clean grains as they floated. Soon the whole troop had learned the trick.

↑ *Japanese macaques groom each other while bathing. In the winter there are few food sources around, and the macaques resort to eating tree bark and buds. They must rely on their reserves of body fat to see them through the winter months.*

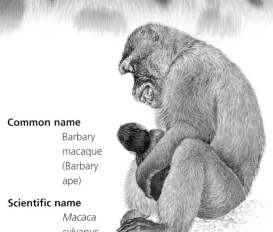

Common name
Barbary macaque (Barbary ape)

Scientific name
Macaca sylvanus

Family Cercopithecidae

Order Primates

Size Length head/body: 22–30 in (55–76 cm). Female about 20% smaller than male

Weight 10–20 lb (4.5–9 kg)

Key features Grayish-brown monkey with almost no tail; face hairless with large cheek pouches to store food

Habits Lives in small groups of up to about 40 animals (usually fewer); spends more time on the ground than other macaques; active during the day

Breeding Single young born at any time of year after gestation period of 210 days. Weaned at about 1 year; females sexually mature at 2–4 years, males at 5–7 years. May live up to about 30 years in captivity, about 20 in the wild

Voice Wide range of typical monkey sounds

Diet Mostly plant material, including fruit and leaves, seeds, shoots, acorns, tubers, bark, and pine needles; some animal food such as insects (especially caterpillars)

Habitat Rocky mountain slopes and montane woodland

Distribution Morocco, Algeria, Tunisia, and Gibraltar

Status Population: about 15,000; IUCN Vulnerable; CITES II. Once found widely across North Africa, but now reduced to a few scattered populations

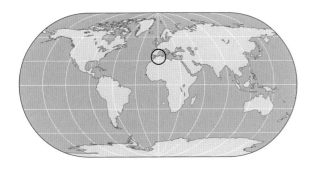

Barbary Macaque

Macaca sylvanus

Lacking a visible tail, Barbary macaques are unusual among monkeys in resembling apes. They are also the only monkeys living wild in Europe.

MOST PEOPLE DEFINE APES AS monkeys without tails, which is the main reason the Barbary macaque is commonly known as the Barbary ape. In fact, it is a monkey, and it does have a tail, although it is a very short one. The Barbary macaque, as it is more correctly known, is unusual in other ways too. All its close relatives come from Asia, and it is the only macaque to live in Africa. In addition, it is the only primate, apart from humans, to live wild in Europe, although it is uncertain whether or not its presence there is entirely natural. The most famous colony of Barbary macaques, living on the Rock of Gibraltar (at the southern tip of Spain), is also one of the smallest. Some scientists believe that the Gibralter animals are descended from macaques whose fossils have been found elsewhere in Europe. Others insist that they were imported from Africa long after their European ancestors had become extinct.

Old Superstition

Whatever their origins, the Barbary macaques of Gibraltar are secure: The population has been boosted by introductions from Africa, notably during World War II, when the Gibraltar macaques were reduced to only seven animals. An old superstition warned that if Gibraltar's macaques died out, Britain would lose the Rock from its collection of colonies. So Prime Minister Winston Churchill arranged for more to be transported from Africa to boost local morale.

The lucky hundred or so macaques in Gibraltar are well looked after, but life for their relatives in North Africa is not so rosy. They live in pine and oak forests on the slopes of the Atlas Mountains. Some have retreated to the

 SEE ALSO Orangutans **4:**14; Gorilla, Mountain **4:**20; Macaque, Japanese **4:**48

high cedar forests, while their lowland home has been taken over for human use. Many forest areas have been cleared for agriculture or the trees felled for charcoal. In places Barbary macaques are forced to live 6,500 feet (2,000 m) above sea level. Others live on degraded slopes, overgrazed by countless sheep and goats. Some live in semidesert or in coastal scrub, eking out a living as best they can. Barbary macaques eat a wide variety of foods and supplement their natural diet of leaves, fruit, and acorns by raiding crops from fields and by stealing stored food meant for humans. Not surprisingly, the monkeys are unpopular, and they end up losing their homes, and sometimes their lives, to the farmers. The numbers of Barbary macaques and their geographical range have been severely reduced in recent times. They now occur only in the Middle Atlas Mountains and a few localities in Morocco and Algeria.

⊕ Male Barbary macaques sometimes use babies to appease aggression by dominant males. When threatened, a male will pick up a baby and present it to the aggressor, whose behavior switches to huddling and chattering over the infant.

Unprotected

The home range of a Barbary macaque troop may be as small as 65 acres (26 ha) where there is plenty of food, but in other places they may roam over more than 3,000 acres (1,200 ha). They live in small social groups of up to 40 animals with a strict hierarchy within the group.

It takes about four years for Barbary macaques to begin to breed. A mother devotes an entire year to raising her single youngster, often assisted by the males in the troop. The monkeys breed slowly, so populations take a long time to recover from losses. All primates are automatically listed on Appendix II of CITES, restricting international trade, but the Barbary macaque suffers little from that problem and is not given special protection. The best way to conserve Barbary macaques would be to preserve their habitat. But in a region where the need to feed an ever-increasing human population is putting so much pressure on land for farming, it is going to be a difficult task to achieve.

Common name Black macaque (Celebes macaque, Sulawesi crested macaque)

Scientific name *Macaca nigra*

Family Cercopithecidae

Order Primates

Size Length head/body: male 20–22 in (51–56 cm); female 18–20 in (46–51 cm); tail length: 1 in (2 cm)

Weight Male 20–22 lb (9–10 kg); female 12–15.5 lb (5–7 kg)

Key features Coat black, with prominent pink sitting pads (ischeal callosities); long, black face with prominent ridges down side of nose; hair on head rises to a stiff crest; tail is of little use

Habits Active during the day; lives in troops; forages on the ground as well as in trees

Breeding Single infant born after gestation period of 5.5 months. Weaned at 1 year; females sexually mature at 3–4 years, males at 4–5 years. May live up to about 30 years in captivity, 20 in the wild

Voice Loud screams

Diet Fruit; also young leaves, buds, invertebrates (such as caterpillars), and birds' eggs; sometimes raids crops

Habitat Tropical forest and areas of regrowth

Distribution Sulawesi (Indonesia)

Status Population: about 144,000; IUCN Endangered; CITES II. Threatened due to logging activities and hunting

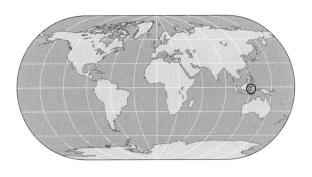

Black Macaque

Macaca nigra

Black macaques are large, relatively peaceful monkeys that live in the lush rain forests of Sulawesi. Despite being a threatened species, they are eaten as a delicacy on the Indonesian island.

THE BLACK OR CELEBES MACAQUE lives in Indonesia, just north of the equator. It is restricted to the northeastern corner of Sulawesi (which used to be known as Celebes) and other adjacent islands. The black macaque is also known as the Sulawesi crested macaque. The name refers to the punklike crest of hair sported by both males and females. It is known as the black macaque because it is basically black all over, with a few white-tipped hairs and pink "sitting patches" on its buttocks. The face is black, long, and narrow, with an elongated snout, a prominent brow, and high, bony cheek ridges. The tail is just a tiny stump.

Troop Life

Black macaques, like other macaques, live in social groups. They usually number about five to 25 individuals, but occasionally when troops merge, there can be up to 100 animals. Females form the stable core of the troop, since they tend to stay with the same troop into which they were born. The males, however, leave when they reach sexual maturity, then spend their lives moving from troop to troop.

As in other macaques, the troop has a social structure that is determined by the hierarchy of the individuals. In females rank is inherited, but males have to compete. Because the males move from troop to troop, their hierarchy level can change depending on social environment. Within the troop black macaques recognize each other and acknowledge rank. When two animals meet, they embrace head to tail and sniff each other's genitals, just as dogs do. Bonds between females and between

females and their offspring are particularly close. Social grooming takes up a large amount of time and helps strengthen social links. Even males generally interact on friendly terms. Black macaques are less aggressive than most other macaque species.

⊕ *A black macaque feeding on figs. Black macaques are known to feed on over 120 species of wild plant, and will supplement their diet with delicacies such as caterpillars and birds' eggs.*

Communication within the group is visual and vocal. Black macaques use loud scream calls, particularly when confronted by another troop. A dominant male will also use calls to stop troop members fighting. Black macaques have a variety of facial expressions. Staring with an open mouth and lip-smacking are both signs of aggression. To demonstrate submission, a "fear grimace" is adopted.

Black macaques are omnivores and eat a wide range of plant and animal foods. Most of their diet consists of plant material, mainly fruits and berries, but also young leaves, flowers, and buds. They are known to use at least 120 species of wild plants, but will also sometimes raid farmers' crops for fruit, vegetables, and corn.

Storage Pouches

The troop spends a large proportion of the day traveling through its patch of rain forest looking for food. The animals have large cheek pouches that can hold as much food as the stomach. When foraging, they stuff their cheek pouches as full as possible, then retire to a safer spot to chew and swallow. They also have powerful jaws and large back teeth, which they use as nutcrackers to break open tough seeds and fruits. The macaques generally forage in the trees. They also spend time on the ground, where they usually walk on all fours.

When they are ready to breed, the females develop bright-pink, swollen buttocks. Infants are born with their eyes closed at first, but they open within two hours. The infant clings tightly to its mother's belly and stays close to her for the first few months of life. It then gradually becomes more adventurous and spends more time playing with other group members. The bond between mother and infant lasts as long as it stays in the group (for life in the case of females), but adult males also take great interest in the welfare of the offspring. With male young the bond lasts until they become sexually mature, at which point the adults force them to leave the troop and seek a new group.

Numbers of black macaques are falling rapidly. Some estimates claim that 75 percent of the population has disappeared within 15 years. Human activities, including cultivation and logging, reduce the amount of forest available for them. The macaques are also hunted or shot when they raid fields. Many are caught in snares to be sold as bushmeat: Black macaque is considered a delicacy in Sulawesi and is eaten on special occasions. Many are also sold for the pet trade. Consequently, there are thought to be fewer than 150,000 left in the wild.

Common name Savanna baboon (yellow baboon)

Scientific name *Papio cynocephalus*

Family	Cercopithecidae
Order	Primates
Size	Length head/body: male 31–45 in (79–114 cm); female 20–28 in (51–71 cm); tail length: 18–27 in (46–68 cm)
	Weight Male 48–66 lb (22–30 kg); female 24–33 lb (11–15 kg)
Key features	Coat yellowish-gray; shiny black patch of bare skin over buttocks; eyes set close together with prominent brow-ridge above; long, ridged muzzle; powerful jaws with long canine teeth in adult males
Habits	Active during the day; forages on the ground and in trees; lives in large troops averaging 30–40 members
Breeding	Usually single baby born every 1–2 years at any time of year after gestation period of 6 months. Weaned at 1 year; females sexually mature at 5 years, males at 7 years. May live up to about 40 years in captivity, 20–30 in the wild
Voice	Barks, grunts, screeches, yelps, and clicks
Diet	Grass, fruit, seeds, bulbs, lichen, mushrooms, insects, young ungulates, and crops
Habitat	Savanna grassland, open woodland and forest edge, rocky hill country, and semidesert with some grass and thorn bush
Distribution	Widespread in central and eastern Africa
Status	Population: unknown—at least tens of thousands; IUCN Lower Risk: near threatened; CITES II. Fairly common primate

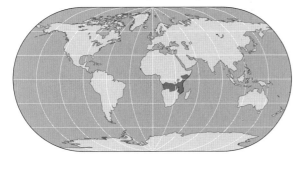

Savanna Baboon

Papio cynocephalus

Savanna baboons owe their success to their complex social structure and adaptability. They eat a wide range of foods, and their flexibility helps them cope with shortages during the dry season.

THE SAVANNA BABOON IS A powerful animal. It has sturdy limbs, and males are considerably larger than females. The arms of a baboon are longer than the legs, so the back slopes downward from the shoulders when the animal is walking on all fours. The adult's tail has a pronounced kink, owing to the first three or four tail bones becoming joined together, giving it a hooked shape. The coat is coarse and brindled yellow-brown, hence the animal's other name of "yellow baboon." As in all baboons, the muzzle is long, giving it a somewhat dog-shaped face (its Latin name, *cynocephalus*, means "dog head.") The long muzzle houses powerful jaws, with large molars for grinding tough plant food. Adult males possess big canine fangs that are 2 inches (5 cm) long. The bare skin of the face is black, with sparse white hairs. There is also black skin on the hands, feet, ears, rump, and scrotum. The hands are wide and strong, with stubby digits and fully opposable thumbs to allow gripping.

Highly Social

Savanna baboons live in large, sociable troops of between eight and 200 animals, although 30 to 40 is most usual. Baboon social life is extremely complex, with subtle (and sometimes not so subtle) relationships between individuals established and maintained by an elaborate communication system of calls and expressions. Good communication is vital for surviving the day-to-day pressures of baboon life, in which animals need to avoid predators, establish hierarchies within the troop, and compete with other troops for space and food.

 SEE ALSO Lion **2**:14; Leopard **2**:30; Hyena, Spotted **2**:108; Baboon, Hamadryas **4**:58

⊖ *A male baboon in Tsavo, Kenya, showing the prominent ridges on the long, doglike muzzle. The muzzle houses powerful jaws with large molar teeth.*

The females form the core of each troop, and they stay with the same group, in the same home range, throughout their life. Within the females of a troop there is a strict and stable hierarchy of dominance. Daughters of a high-ranking female are automatically high ranking themselves. Within a family the youngest daughters rank highly, and by the age of two and a half a female's rank is fixed for life. Hierarchy and social status are just as important among the males, but are more flexible. Males achieve high status by strength and by forming alliances with other males. Young males leave the troop in which they were born, usually around the age of four, and join another troop. They may change troops several times in their lives: Each time they have to go through the process of becoming accepted and climbing the hierarchy, since high rank gains the prize of mating with more females.

Just Good Friends

Male baboons often make close "friendships" with a chosen female. A female may have between one and three such "friends," with whom she spends a lot of time. She will groom them attentively, forage with them, and sleep nearby. Such friends behave well toward her offspring, even if they are not its father. They hold, carry, and groom the baby baboon, share food, and protect it from bullying by other troop members. In return, the male friends are more likely than other troop members to be favored when the female is receptive and ready to mate.

Friendships and paternal behavior also have other benefits for the males. If a male is being threatened by a higher-ranking male, holding out a baby will usually inhibit an attack. Males also make alliances with each other, and two subordinate males acting together can often chase off an otherwise dominant male. All the males in the troop will unite if they meet a rival group of baboons. Then there is likely to be a serious confrontation, since competition for good living areas is always intense.

Varied Diet

All baboons are omnivores, which means they eat a wide range of both plant and animal food. Plants make up the bulk of their diet, especially grasses, fruit, and seeds, particularly of acacia trees. The animals also eat buds, shoots, flowers, and bark. In the dry season they cope better than many other animals, since they use their powerful hands to dig up juicy bulbs and tubers. They will also dig for water in dry streambeds. They supplement their diet with invertebrates such as mopane grubs, spiders, grasshoppers, and occasionally even scorpions. They also eat lizards, turtles, frogs, fish, and birds' eggs and nestlings. Crocodile eggs are eagerly dug up and consumed. Rodents, hares, and even young gazelles may be captured if they are found in the long grass. Baboons are unpopular with farmers, since they kill young goats and sheep and also raid crops.

When hunting, savanna baboons use a simple form of cooperation, spreading out and "flushing out" prey. However, animals that catch anything share food only reluctantly. When foraging, groups can travel considerable distances depending on the quality of the habitat and the season. In the wet season, when food is plentiful, they will cover 2.8 miles (4.5 km) in an average day, but during the dry

Baboon Communication

Communication between animals is very important within such a tightly knit society. Baboons use a variety of calls, postures, and facial expressions to convey messages to each other. Aggression toward another baboon is demonstrated by tooth grinding. A subordinate withdrawing from a conflict will adopt a facial expression known as a "fear grimace," with the mouth open, often accompanied by short yakking calls. During courtship baboons make a muffled growl with the mouth nearly closed and cheeks puffing in and out. Infants use a chirplike clicking sound and have a special "ick-ooer" noise that they use when rebuffed.

season they often need to travel 3.7 miles (6 km). The distances may be halved if their habitat is lush, but doubled in poor regions. The size of the home range depends on the size of the group and the quality of their habitat, and can be between 0.75 and 15.5 square miles (2 and 40 sq. km). The troop travels from one feeding patch to another. The dominant males decide where to go and are aggressive toward troop members that lag behind.

When foraging, the group is spread out, but individuals will still maintain contact with each other. A typical foraging posture is sitting on the ground, searching for food with the

⊕ *Baboons often make loud coughs and grunts: Communication is vital to this highly sociable primate species.*

hands, then shuffling forward when one piece of ground has been covered.

On the African savanna there are many creatures that will prey on baboons if they get a chance. Lions, hyenas, and leopards are the biggest threat—even to adults—and eagles and jackals will take young baboons. By sticking together, animals in a troop are much safer. There are many pairs of eyes to watch out for trouble; and if a predator is spotted, loud calls will alert the rest of the troop. The males will then move toward the source of danger, and their threatening postures and attacks will make most predators retreat. At an alarm call baboons rush for cover to the nearest trees, with young males bringing up the rear guard.

Baboons are most vulnerable to attack at night, so the troop usually chooses the safest possible place to sleep, on high ledges or among tree branches. Here leopards are the greatest threat, since they are nocturnal and can climb well. However, the baboons have a way of deterring any animal prowling below—they bombard it with liquid excrement.

Irresistible Youngsters

Savanna baboons can breed at any time of the year, but births tend to peak during the rainy seasons, when food is most plentiful. When females are receptive, the skin around their genital region swells and becomes bright pink. In that condition they are very attractive to

males and may mate with many different partners. After a gestation period of six months a single infant is born (twins are rare), usually at night. Babies have black fur and red faces, and seem to be irresistible to adults, who try to examine, touch, and carry the youngsters.

At first the baby is completely dependent on its mother, spending all its time hanging onto her belly and suckling. After about a month it begins to move independently, and by two months it is able to walk and clamber over logs. After about six weeks it rides on its mother's back, and by the time it is three to four months old a baby baboon plays with other infants. It will start to eat solid food and by now can climb reasonably well, but still takes milk from its mother. It is weaned after one year, but still relies on its mother for guidance and protection until it is nearly two years old.

⬆ A baboon family group engaged in social activities: One youngster grabs another's tail. Baby baboons are a source of interest to the adults of the troop, who pay them special attention.

⬅ A Chacma baboon troop at a drinking pool in the Okavango Delta, Botswana. The five species of baboon used to be classified as one single species. They all look very similar, with the males boasting a thick mane of fur around the shoulders.

Common name Hamadryas baboon (sacred baboon)

Scientific name *Papio hamadryas*

Family Cercopithecidae

Order Primates

Size Length head/body: male 27.5–37 in (70–95 cm); female 20–25.5 in (50–65 cm); tail length: 16.5–24 in (42–60 cm)

Weight Male 37–55.5 lb (17–25 kg); female 22–29.5 lb (10–13 kg)

Key features Dull-brown to silver-gray coat with longer hair over shoulders, especially in adult males; red patch of skin over hips and naked red face with prominent side ridges on long muzzle

Habits Terrestrial; walks on all fours; lives in bands of males, each with a harem of females; bands come together to sleep

Breeding Usually a single baby born after gestation period of 5–6 months. Weaned at around 1 year; females sexually mature at 3.5 years, males at 2 years. May live up to about 40 years in captivity, 30–40 in the wild

Voice Variety of barks and grunts

Diet Grass, fruit, seeds, bulbs, insects, hares, and young ungulates; sometimes raids crops

Habitat Arid subdesert, steppe, and bare highlands

Distribution Northeastern Sudan, eastern Ethiopia, and northern Somalia; also east of Red Sea in Yemen and Saudi Arabia

Status Population: likely to be in the thousands; IUCN Lower Risk: near threatened; CITES II. A vulnerable species

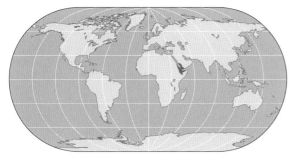

Hamadryas Baboon

Papio hamadryas

Hamadryas baboons live in unusual, complex societies. Males form the stable core of the large troops, and each has a small harem of females. The hamadryas was once the sacred baboon of Egypt, but has now been exterminated there.

HAMADRYAS BABOONS HAVE A build similar to other baboons, with a relatively stocky body and a long, doglike muzzle. Their most characteristic feature is the coat, which in mature, sexually active males is long and silver-gray, with a heavy cape covering the neck and shoulders. The hair is lighter on the cheeks and tail tip and around the edges of the sitting pads of the buttocks. Young animals and maturing females are brown. All have hairless, pinkish-red skin on the face and sitting patches. As in other baboons, the males are much larger than the females.

Male-Centered Social Life

The social life and organization of the hamadryas baboon is unusual among monkeys in that it is centered around males. It is the males that form the stable groups and stick to one home range, while the females move between them. That is the reverse of what is normal among most monkey societies.

The hamadryas social structure is arranged in four levels. The smallest unit is a male with a small harem of females (usually two to five) and their offspring. Two or three of these single-male groups join to form a clan. The males of such clans are usually closely related and often work as a team. When traveling, the younger male leads, while the older male brings up the rear guard. Clans join together to form bands of 30 to 90 (averaging 60) animals. The bands usually travel and forage together. At night large numbers of bands come together to sleep. These troops often number more than 100 animals and can be as large as 750.

Each male maintains strict discipline within his harem. He must keep his group together and will use force, usually a bite to the nape of the neck, if one of his females strays. He will also fight other males to gain or retain females. Fighting males fence with open jaws and hit out with their hands, but almost never make physical contact and so tend to avoid injury.

When a male becomes sexually mature, he leaves the unit in which he was born, but stays within the same clan. He attracts or kidnaps females to start his own harem.

The unusual multilevel social organization has arisen because of two conflicting factors: The baboons' sleeping sites (rocky outcrops and cliffs) are scarce, so they need to come together in large troops to make the most of them. However, their food is widely dispersed, so the animals are better off in small groups that can forage apart. The baboons can travel considerable distances when foraging—between 4 and 12 miles (6 and 19 km) a day.

⤵ *The primary social unit of hamadryas society is the harem of one male and up to five females. The females will show aggression toward each other over gaining the male's attention and will fight for the right to groom him.*

A Sacred Animal

The hamadryas was the sacred baboon of the ancient Egyptians. It was often shown in pictures and carvings on the walls of temples and other buildings as the attendant or representative of Thoth, the god of letters and the scribe of the gods. Free-living baboons in the temple of Thoth were regarded as priests. Baboons were also mummified and entombed with high-ranking people. The sacred baboons were also associated with sun worship. Hamadryas baboons are increasingly coming into conflict with people as more and more areas of their natural distribution are used for cultivation. The baboons have now been exterminated in Egypt, even though they were once considered sacred there. But in other parts of their range numbers are increasing. In Saudi Arabia, where they are the only nonhuman primate in the wild, they are a common sight in cities, particularly near garbage dumps.

Common name
Mandrill

Scientific name
Mandrillus sphinx

Family Cercopithecidae

Order Primates

Size Length head/body: 22–37 in (55–95 cm); tail length: 2–3 in (5–8 cm)

Weight Male 42–66 lb (19–30 kg); female 22–33 lb (10–15 kg)

Key features Olive-brown, heavily built baboon; male has a brightly colored face and posterior

Habits Lives in small, male-dominated groups; active during the day, mostly on the ground; retires to trees at night to sleep

Breeding Single young born at intervals of 1–2 years after gestation period of 175 days. Weaned at 1 year; sexually mature at 4–5 years. May live more than 45 years in captivity, probably many fewer in the wild

Voice Individuals often silent; larger groups are noisy, making chorus of double barks; sometimes grunts and squeals

Diet Prefers fruits, but will eat almost anything, including small animals

Habitat Mainly evergreen coastal forest

Distribution Equatorial West Africa

Status Population: unknown, but declining; IUCN Vulnerable; CITES I

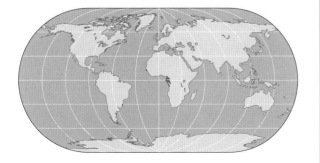

Mandrill

Mandrillus sphinx

The large and spectacular mandrill is famed for its vivid colors. However, it is seriously threatened in its natural home, where it is regarded as a valuable source of bushmeat.

THE MALE MANDRILL HAS TO be one of the most impressive of all primates. It has a high, hairy crest on its head and a thick mane around its neck, giving it a powerful appearance. Its long muzzle has prominent ridges that are a bright, electric blue, with a crimson stripe between them. The general fur color is a drab brown, but the mandrill has red nostrils, orange cheeks, an orange beard, and blue ears. The rear end is no less spectacular, with areas of bare skin colored with bright red, white, and blue.

Social Rank

The colorful fur and skin are signs of social rank and develop progressively with increasing age. The purpose of the spectacular facial adornments is to ensure that the animals know who is boss—a useful skill in the gloomy light of the dense rain forest. If the dominant group leader can be recognized at a glance, fighting is much reduced, since other males will not challenge his authority by mistake.

Mandrills live in small groups of up to 30 animals, led by single dominant male. There are often two or more subordinate males present, whose size and coloring are less pronounced than in the group leader. The rest of the group are mostly breeding females and their recent offspring. The groups are extremely vocal and often call noisily to each other. But old males—probably those displaced from the social groups—generally feed alone and are silent. Overall, adult males are uncommon. The stress that goes with maintaining dominance probably contributes to the high rate of mortality.

Mandrills can climb well and retire to the trees to sleep each night. They are normally active only during the daytime and mostly

forage on the ground. They will eat almost anything edible, but prefer fruit whenever it is available. In seasons with abundant fruit large groups of mandrills, perhaps amounting to several hundred, may gather to feed in the same area. The mandrills' diet also includes leaves, roots, fungi, land crabs, and snails. Sometimes they catch lizards, mice, and even small antelope. Mandrills generally travel about 5 miles (8 km) in the course of a day, but they can roam twice as far if they need to. The dominant male usually takes up the rear; but if danger threatens, he will move to the front. Mandrills feed intensively in one place for about a week, turning over stones and inspecting debris for potential food. When supplies start to become scarce, they move on, covering an area of about 18 square miles (50 sq. km) in a year.

Both sexes reach sexual maturity at four or five years. However, the males are unlikely to breed until they are much older, being kept from doing so by the group's leader. Females are pregnant for about six months and give birth to a single offspring. The young stick close to their mother for a year or more and also enjoy protection from the rest of the group.

Continuous destruction of the forest means that mandrills are always under pressure, having fewer and fewer areas in which to live. In addition, mandrill meat is highly valued among local people, and commercial hunters have wiped out many mandrill groups. Those living near roads are especially vulnerable. In the daytime the animals are hunted using dogs and guns. At night they can be shot in the trees, illuminated by spotlights as they sleep. Refrigerated trucks carry the meat to distant markets. Today there are a few protected reserves to conserve the wildlife of West African tropical forests. It is hoped that there are enough mandrills left in safe areas to prevent the species from dying out altogether.

⊕ *A captive male mandrill in a zoo. The blue part of the face is always swollen, so the animal looks permanently fierce. The wide gape and huge teeth are also impressive.*

Common name Gelada
baboon

Scientific name
Theropithecus gelada

Family Cercopithe-
cidae

Order Primates

Size Length head/body:
20–30 in (50–75 cm); tail
length: 13–22 in (32–55 cm).
Male generally bigger than
female

Weight Male 33–48 lb (15–22 kg);
female 22–33 lb (10–15 kg)

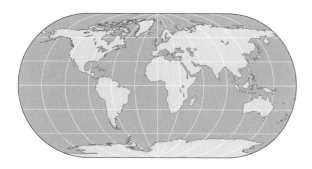

Key features Large, ground-dwelling monkey
with long brown fur that makes it look
thickset and very heavy; adult males
develop flowing cape of paler hair around
shoulders and forelegs and conspicuous
patches of naked skin on chest

Habits Terrestrial; lives in groups on open grassland
and cliff ledges; active during the day

Breeding Single young born every 2 years in
February–April after gestation period of 6
months. Weaned at 2 years, females sexually
mature at 3–4 years, males at 8 years. May
live 30 years in captivity, about 15–20 in the
wild

Voice Grunts and screams, depending on
circumstances; alarm call is a loud bark

Diet Mostly grass

Habitat High-altitude rocky cliffs and gorges above
5,000 ft (1,500 m)

Distribution Confined to northern Ethiopia

Status Population: fewer than 500,000; IUCN Lower
Risk: near threatened; CITES II

Gelada Baboon

Theropithecus gelada

*The unique gelada baboon is found only on the high
plateau of Ethiopia, where it lives along precipitous
cliff edges. It is threatened by continued expansion
of farming and human activities.*

GELADAS HAVE A UNIQUE ground-dwelling, grass-
eating way of life that makes them different
from other types of baboons. They live at high
altitudes above the tree line and have no access
to trees large enough for them to climb.
Consequently, they are the only species of
monkey that spends all its time on the ground.

Grass Eaters

Where the geladas live, high on the Ethiopian
plateau far away from trees, there is no fruit to
eat. So the gelada has become the only type of
monkey that feeds almost entirely on grass. It
does not need to move far to find grass and sits
around all day on its haunches, picking its food
by hand. Geladas will sometimes also eat roots,
especially during the dry season when the grass
is brown and withered. Roots are dug up or
wrenched from the ground, leaving large areas
of bare soil and overturned turf. Geladas
occasionally eat a few insects, but probably only
by accident along with the grass.

Geladas live in rocky places more than
5,000 feet (1,500 m) above sea level. They
gather together at dusk along the tops of cliffs
and steep slopes, moving down to sleep on
rocky ledges where rock faces and ravines
provide shelter from the rain and wind. Geladas
rarely venture more than a mile or so (2 km)
from the cliffs and flee to the safety of their
ledges if threatened. Sleeping on ledges also
makes them relatively safe from most predators
except leopards, but these cats are now rare.

Geladas live in large and complex social
groups, each dominated by a single adult male.
Males that have no harem gather into bachelor

groups. Adult males have a flowing cape of long hair. Like other baboons, geladas use exaggerated yawns and various displays to establish dominance and access to breeding females. They also peel back their upper lip in a sneering smile to reveal bright- pink gums, forming a greeting display that is unique to the gelada. The dominant males also have a conspicuous bright patch of bare, pink skin in the middle of their chest, which is flashed as part of their social displays.

Cliff-Top Foragers

Geladas come up from their sleeping ledges to the cliff tops and open plateau as soon as the sun rises each morning. They disperse into small groups to seek food, but keep in touch with soft grunts. However, at any point some of the animals are keeping a lookout for danger, particularly large birds of prey. A sharp warning bark will send the geladas running for the safety of the nearest crags.

In the past humans have not seriously threatened geladas, since there were relatively few people sharing the cold highlands where they live. Some geladas were occasionally shot to collect their impressive cape skins to make ceremonial cloaks. Although few geladas were killed, a high proportion of the best breeding males were taken—a serious threat to the population as a whole. Fortunately, the gelada's high-altitude, rocky habitat is unattractive for agricultural development. Nevertheless, expansion of fields and villages is a threat. For a brief period geladas were trapped and taken to the United States for use in medical research, but the practice has now ceased.

As late as the 1970s there were probably at least half a million geladas in Ethiopia. They are relatively safe within protected areas, such as the Simien National Park and parts of the Blue Nile Gorge. Nevertheless, the gelada's restricted distribution means that there is always a risk that disease or another misfortune could quickly reduce numbers to a critical level. Drought is a frequent problem in Ethiopia, and the geladas' limited food supplies are eaten by increasing numbers of cattle and goats.

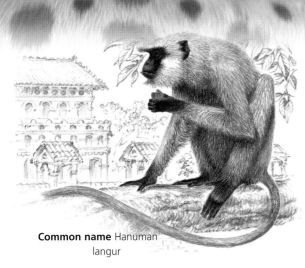

Common name Hanuman langur

Scientific name *Semnopithecus entellus*

Family Cercopithecidae

Order Primates

Size Length head/body: 16–31 in (41–78 cm); tail length: 27–42.5 in (69–108 cm)

Weight Male 20–66 lb (9–30 kg); female 16.5–40 lb (7.5–18 kg)

Key features Slender, agile monkey with a long tail; upperparts gray, brown, or buff; crown and underparts white or yellowish; black face, ears, hands, and feet; prominent brow ridge

Habits Active by day in small social groups that are dominated by 1 or more males; forages on ground as well as in trees

Breeding Usually a single offspring born after gestation period of 190–210 days. Weaned at 10–12 months; females sexually mature at 3–4 years, males at 6–7 years. May live about 25 years in captivity, 15 in the wild

Voice Resonant whoops and guttural alarm calls

Diet Mainly leaves; also some fruits, seeds, flowers, and sometimes crops

Habitat Varied: includes wet tropical forests, shrubs, desert edges, alpine scrub, and urban areas

Distribution From Pakistan through Himalayas to Nepal and Bangladesh; India and Sri Lanka

Status Population: probably about half a million; Indian population estimated at 233,800 (1986); IUCN Lower Risk: near threatened; CITES I

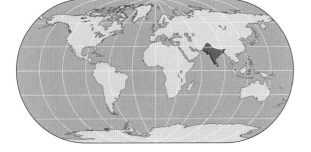

Hanuman Langur

Semnopithecus entellus

Hanuman langurs live sociable, relatively peaceful lives. Named after the Hindu monkey-god, they are considered sacred in India and are allowed to steal food and raid crops unhindered.

HANUMAN LANGURS ARE THE most widespread of all the leaf-eating monkeys, living throughout a huge part of the Indian subcontinent. They are flexible in the type of habitat in which they can survive. They can be found from sea level to over 13,000 feet (4,000 m), in habitats as diverse as rain forests, alpine scrub, semidesert, and even in villages and towns. Even so, their populations are still threatened, since their preferred forest habitats are being cut down.

Unlike most other langurs, Hanuman langurs spend much of their time on the ground—as much as 80 percent of the day in nonforested areas. When on the ground, they sometimes run using all four feet, instead of walking upright. Up in the trees they are extremely agile and can make horizontal leaps of 10 to 16.5 feet (3 to 5 m) or diagonal falling leaps of up to 43 feet (13 m).

Laid-back Lifestyle

Langur social life is relatively calm, compared to the bickering and chattering of guenons and macaques. Most animals belong to a social group, although some individuals may live alone. Males are always the leaders and defenders of a group, but the structure varies depending on the habitat. Where there is plenty of food, mixed-sex groups may include several adult males. The males are tolerant of each other once their relative status has been established. Normal group size is 13 to 37, but groups will come together for feeding or drinking, resulting in gatherings of over 100 animals. When groups meet, there is usually no aggression. Langurs make small, appeasing

 SEE ALSO Baboon, Hamadryas **4:**58; Mandrill **4:**60; Monkey, Black-and-White Colobus **4:**68; Monkey, Proboscis **4:**70

noises to each other, which seem to minimize tension between them.

Where there is more competition for food supplies, the social structure is different. In such cases there is usually only one male per group of females, with an average of two adult females per male. They live together with an assortment of juveniles. The resident male will fight off any other males that try to join the group. Remaining males wander alone or form "bachelor groups" of up to 30 or so animals.

Once males have established a dominance hierarchy by fighting, the structure of the group is generally stable. A lower-ranking male will reaffirm his subordinate position to the dominant male by approaching him and "presenting"—turning his hindquarters toward him in a sign of submission. He will then lie on the ground while the dominant male grooms him. On the rare occasions that a dominant male is challenged, he stares at the subordinate, slaps the ground, and grunts and grimaces. Suddenly, he lunges and chases his challenger, hitting and even biting him.

Within a group females have an established hierarchy, but it is weak. Expressions of dominance and submission between females are rare, although a dominant female will occasionally slap a lower-ranking one.

Tough at the Top

For a male, life at the top as troop leader is usually short—two or three years is average. The lead male will eventually be ousted from his position by a younger rival. Alternatively, a younger male may split a group by stealing some females to form a troop of his own. If a young male succeeds in taking over a group, he often attempts to kill all the young, since losing their babies brings the females back into breeding condition. He can then mate with them, giving him a chance to father as many

⊕ *A Hanuman langur mother rocks her baby. Newborn Hanuman langurs are chocolate brown, in contrast to the silvery gray of the adults.*

offspring as possible in his short time as leader. The females are protective of their young and will gang together to defend their smallest babies. Juvenile males in the group, who offer a potential threat to the new leader's authority, are chased away. Those that survive form bachelor gangs until they are old enough to claim their own females.

Despite the occasional power struggle, day-to-day life within a Hanuman langur troop is generally calm. Even when they meet other species of monkeys, langurs are just as peaceful as within their own groups. They often form mixed troops with the much more aggressive macaques. Because the two types of monkey feed on different things, there is little or no competition between them.

Like all langurs, Hanuman langurs are almost entirely vegetarian. To cope with their poor diet of tough leaves they have a complex pouched stomach. The first two pouches are

Sacred Animals

In India many troops of Hanuman langurs live in close contact with humans in or around villages, towns, and cities. They scavenge for food, raid gardens, orchards, and crops, and even help themselves to fruit and vegetables from market stalls. Because they are considered to be sacred animals, their brash behavior is tolerated. They are often seen in the company of traveling holy men, who share some of the food donated to them with their monkey companions.

fermentation chambers where bacteria break down the tough plant cell walls and help neutralize toxins. Hanuman langurs eat many poisonous plants that other animals avoid.

Cross-Country Foraging

Leaves are not a rich food source, so langurs need to eat large quantities to obtain enough sustenance. In dense forests finding enough food is not usually a problem, but in less well-vegetated areas groups may have to forage over several miles every day. The size of the home range depends on the size of the group and the type and quality of the habitat. In forests, where food is abundant, mixed-sex groups of five to 15 individuals use relatively small home ranges, which can be as little as 42 acres (17 ha). In drier regions groups can consist of 30 or more animals that forage over much larger areas, typically 5 square miles (13 sq. km). All-male groups, whose travel is not constrained by the presence of slow youngsters, can cover ranges of 2.7 to 8.5 square miles (7 to 22 sq. km).

Each home range may overlap with those of other groups, but will tend to have a core area into which other groups do not wander. Boundaries are not enforced. Instead, the males use a deep, resonant whooping call, often in a morning chorus, that keeps groups spaced comfortably apart.

Hanuman langurs are most active in early morning and late afternoon, sleeping during the middle of the day. At night the group sleeps together in a tree, gathering at the thinner ends of branches away from large predators like leopards and tigers. In ranges with no trees the troop will sleep huddled on high rocks.

Mating can occur throughout the year; but in areas that experience seasonal rains, most births happen during the dry season. The female initiates mating by looking at the male and presenting her rear to let him know that she is fertile. She will object violently if he ignores her and may even bite him.

The female gives birth seven months after mating, usually to a single offspring. Newborn

babies are dark brown, in contrast to the silver-gray fur of the adults. Soon after birth the other females in the troop show great interest in the newborn baby and will pick it up, pass it around, and some may even suckle the infant. Small babies are extremely vulnerable to predators and accidental injury. In urban areas the most common cause of death for all langurs—but especially the perpetually curious youngsters—is electrocution from pylons and wiring on house roofs. The mother's nursing instinct is strong; and if a baby dies, she will carry the body around with her for days, trying to encourage it to cling and suckle. For the first eight months babies are totally dependent on their mother's milk. As a baby grows, its dark fur becomes progressively lighter, and the youngster becomes less dependent on its mother. Weaning takes place at about 10 to 12 months, after which the female becomes fertile and ready to mate again.

Growing Up

Young females generally stay within the group into which they were born. They often help their mothers with younger offspring, until they themselves become sexually mature at three or four years old. Young males spend a great deal of time playing games such as "king of the hill" and fighting. Such games become trials of strength through which the animals determine their social position. Males leave their troop at three to five years of age, usually when a new adult male takes over. When sexually mature at six or seven years, the young males begin to look for their own females.

↑ *Hanuman langurs foraging for food. Although mainly tree dwelling, the animals can survive in areas where forestation is scarce, moving across the ground on all four feet.*

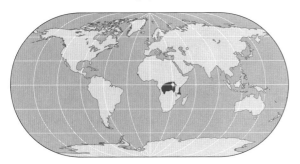

Common name Black-and-white colobus monkey (white-epauleted black colobus monkey, Angola colobus monkey)

Scientific name *Colobus angolensis*

Family Cercopithecidae

Order Primates

Size Length head/body: 20–26 in (50–66 cm); tail length: 25–35 in (63–89 cm)

Weight 20–44 lb (9–20 kg)

Key features Large black monkey with white cheeks and long, flowing white cape around shoulders

Habits Spends almost all its time up in trees; active during the day; lives in small family groups

Breeding One young born every 20 months or so after a gestation period of 6 months. Weaned at about 6 months; females sexually mature at about 4 years, males at 6 years. May live 30 years in captivity, many fewer in the wild

Voice Loud croaking and roaring chorus at dawn and dusk, otherwise generally silent; sometimes makes a loud cough

Diet Mostly leaves, but about a third of its diet consists of fruit and seeds

Habitat Mountain and lowland forests

Distribution Central African forests; scattered localities in Tanzania

Status Fairly common; IUCN Vulnerable (some small, isolated populations); CITES II. Apart from habitat loss, the main threat to colobus monkeys is hunting for their skins, which have been popular with tourists

Black-and-White Colobus Monkey

Colobus angolensis

There are five species of black-and-white colobus monkeys, and Colobus angolensis *is a typical one. It lives in the tropical forests of Africa and remains fairly common, despite habitat loss and hunting for skins.*

COLOBUS MONKEYS ARE SLENDER creatures that look much larger than they actually are. The illusion is created by their characteristic cape of long white hairs around the neck and shoulders. The cheeks and face are also surrounded by long whiskers. The rest of the body is black, although the long tail is often partially white and thick-looking, again because of its long hairs. The black-and-white patterns appear conspicuous in books and photographs, but in the wild the monkeys are extraordinarily easy to overlook as long as they remain still and silent among the treetops.

Variations on Black and White

The five species of colobus monkeys look rather similar. At the same time, they are distinctly different from all other monkeys. Basically, all colobus monkeys are black and white, although the extent of the characteristic white cape and cheeks varies from one species to another. Each species often includes several subspecies, again differentiated by details of their black-and-white pattern. Nevertheless, the animals have similar lifestyles and are all found in a broad band across tropical Africa.

Black-and-white colobus monkeys are able to digest old leaves and coarse vegetable material, and so can live in areas with a distinct dry season. Consequently, unlike the more fussy red colobus monkeys, they can be found in relatively dry forests where the vegetation can be rather indigestible. Red colobus monkeys tend to be found only in rain forests. The black-and-white colobus monkey has also managed to colonize mountain forests in some areas.

daily activity in the trees. They are not continuously active during the day and take frequent rests. They often travel, but will not venture farther than about a third of a mile (500 m). They feed mainly on leaves, which make up about two-thirds of their diet. The rest of their food consists of fruit and seeds. The monkeys chorus again at dusk before settling for the night.

Territorial Truce

Most populations of colobus monkeys live in relatively small social groups. Normally, there is only one fully grown male, but up to six adult females. Such groups use a home range of up to 20 acres (8 ha), part of which may be guarded as a territory from which others of the species are excluded. Territory is usually defended by the adult males, who express hostility to intruders through gestures and exaggerated displays of leaping. Occasionally, territorial behavior is suspended, and several hundred black-and-white colobus monkeys may gather together in the same locality, probably attracted by particularly abundant food.

Females give birth to a single young at any time of the year. The newborn baby weighs about 30 ounces (850 g) and will be suckled by its mother for at least six months. Babies are often handled by individuals other than their mother. Colobus monkeys are highly social creatures and very friendly toward each other. Groups indulge in mutual grooming, combing, and stroking each other's fur.

All colobus species have declined in numbers over the last hundred years or so. Forest clearance for agriculture and human settlement is partly responsible, since fragmented forests make it difficult for the animals to travel from place to place. Hunting for skins is now restricted by law.

⊕ Once the sun is up and the rain has dried from the leaves, black-and-white colobus monkeys begin their daily activities, which take place almost entirely in the trees.

Here the animals tend to grow longer and thicker coats than members of the same species living at lower and warmer altitudes. The black-and-white colobus is principally found between 1,200 and 3,500 feet (365 and 1,066 m) above sea level.

Typically, colobus monkeys make a daily chorus when they wake up around dawn. First they climb into prominent trees or high into the forest canopy. Each group then joins together in a loud session of croaking and roaring as a way of advertising its presence and numbers to others of its species. At the same time, the animals jump around, shaking branches and flicking their tail, while prominently displaying their long white cape. The dominant males tend to make the loudest calls and the most exaggerated movements. They then begin their

Common name Proboscis monkey

Scientific name *Nasalis larvatus*

Family	Cercopithecidae
Order	Primates
Size	Length head/body: male 24–30 in (60–76 cm); female 21–24 in (53–60 cm); tail length: 22–24 in (56–60 cm)
Weight	Male 35–55 lb (16–25 kg); female 15–24 lb (7–11 kg)
Key features	Long, dangling nose in adult males, less developed in females
Habits	Mainly active in late afternoon to dark; lives in small social groups
Breeding	Single young born at any time of year after gestation period of 106 days. Weaned at 7 months; sexually mature at about 3 years. May live up to 23 years in captivity, usually fewer in the wild
Voice	Males make a long, drawn-out resonant honk; female call is a milder sound, similar to that of a goose
Diet	Mainly leaves, but fruit and flowers also eaten when available
Habitat	Found near fresh water in lowland rain forests or mangrove swamps
Distribution	Borneo and Mentawai Islands in the Malay Archipelago
Status	Population: probably fewer than 250,000; IUCN Vulnerable; CITES I. Habitat destruction is threatening populations; hunting is also on the increase

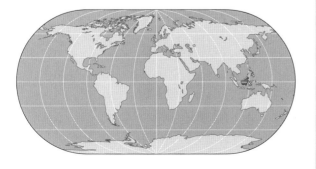

Proboscis Monkey

Nasalis larvatus

The extraordinary-looking proboscis monkey lives in the mangroves and tropical forests of Borneo. It is seriously threatened by human encroachment.

THE PROBOSCIS MONKEY IS A relatively large species of primate that lives in groups of 20 or more individuals. It is found in the mangrove swamps of Borneo and the Mentawai Islands, which lie to the west of Sumatra. Its most outstanding feature is the protruding nose, which hangs down over the mouth in adult males. The nose becomes large and pendulous, and may reach about 3 inches (8 cm) in length. The noses of the young monkeys and the females, however, remain less developed. The purpose of such a large nose in the adult males is unclear. It is thought that the larger the nose, the more attractive the male may be to a female. It has also been suggested that the nose could act as a radiator, helping get rid of some of the excess body heat that the large monkeys generate.

Sound Effects

The nose is known to help produce the loud, resonant "honk" that male proboscis monkeys make. With each vocalization the nose slightly inflates and stiffens, modifying the sound. A warning call in the presence of predators prompts the young to retreat to the forests. Sometimes the sounds are aggressive and made to threaten other members of the group. It is possible that the size of the nose causes subtle changes to the sounds each animal makes, conveying additional information about the size and status of the caller. Juveniles and adult females can make a shrieking sound, which they emit at times of excitement or agitation. In response the adult males may make a low-pitched growling to help restore calm.

As in other primate groups, social grooming is an important means of communication. It also helps reinforce social bonds between individuals. One monkey uses its hands or teeth to groom the coat of another, and each grooming session lasts between one and five minutes.

At birth an infant proboscis monkey has hair that is almost black, while the skin on its face is deep blue. By three months the face will have turned gray, and the black birth coat will become brighter and more like the color of an adult.

⊕ *The pendulous nose of the male proboscis monkey is used in the loud, resonant "honking" sound it makes to warn other proboscis monkeys of predators.*

When fully grown, the proboscis monkey can vary from brown to pale orange on the back, while the underparts are a creamy grayish color.

Excellent Swimmers

Apart from the large nose of the males, another interesting feature of proboscis monkeys is the webbing of skin between their fingers. It is thought to be an adaptation to swimming. Indeed, proboscis monkeys are excellent swimmers, an unusual skill among the primates. The ability to swim, coupled with short fur that dries easily, are probably useful adaptations for the species, since it normally lives in mangroves and swampy lowland forests. The monkeys' trees are often completely surrounded by water for long periods of time, so immersion in the water is likely to be a regular occurrence.

When entering the waters around the coastal regions of Borneo, proboscis monkeys run the risk of being preyed on by crocodiles. The animals therefore prefer to cross rivers at their narrowest points and try to do so in large numbers. Crossing in a group reduces the risk of any one individual being picked out and targeted as prey. Despite their ability to swim, the monkeys mostly stay within the trees. They move carefully from branch to branch, grasping with both their hands and feet. Occasionally, they cross wide gaps by making a great leap from one of the branches, with arms outstretched to grab the next branch.

Proboscis monkeys are strictly vegetarian. Their diet consists mainly of leaves, although they will eat fruit, seeds, and flowers when they are available, as well as the young, soft shoots of the mangroves. Unfortunately for the proboscis monkey, its mangrove swamp habitat is shrinking. Trees have been cut down for human use, and many wet lowland areas have been drained in order to grow crops. Swampy forest that used to be inaccessible to humans is now opened up, exposing the monkeys to hunting. Proboscis monkey populations continue to be broken into smaller groups that may not be viable in the long term.

The New World Monkey Family

Together with the tamarins and marmosets, the New World monkeys (family Cebidae) are the only nonhuman primates found in the Americas. A successful group, cebids live in the evergreen temperate and subtropical forests of Mexico, Central, and southern America from the Amazon Basin to Paraguay, northern Argentina, and southern Brazil. Most are tree-living species that only occasionally come to the ground.

Family Cebidae: 11 genera, 47 species

SQUIRREL MONKEYS 1 genus, 4 species
  Saimiri includes common squirrel monkey (*S. sciureus*); Bolivian squirrel monkey (*S. boliviensis*)

WOOLLY MONKEYS 1 genus, 2 species
  Lagothrix Humboldt's woolly monkey (*L. lagotricha*); yellow-tailed woolly monkey (*L. flavicauda*)

UAKARIS 1 genus, 2 species
  Cacajao red uakari (*C. calvus*); black uakari (*C. melanocephalus*)

NIGHT MONKEYS 1 genus, 2 species
  Aotus northern night monkey (*A. trivirgatus*); southern night monkey (*A. nigriceps*)

SPIDER MONKEYS 1 genus, 6 species
  Ateles includes black-handed spider monkey (*A. geoffroyi*); long-haired spider monkey (*A. belzebuth*)

HOWLER MONKEYS 1 genus, 6 species
  Alouatta includes brown howler monkey (*A. fusca*); mantled howler monkey (*A. palliata*); red howler monkey (*A. seniculus*)

CAPUCHIN MONKEYS 1 genus, 4 species
  Cebus includes brown capuchin (*C. apella*); weeper capuchin (*C. olivaceus*); white-faced capuchin (*C. capucinus*)

SAKI MONKEYS 2 genera, 7 species
  Pithecia 5 species, including monk saki (*P. monachus*); bald-faced saki (*P. irrorata*); buffy saki (*P. albicans*); Guianan saki (*P. pithecia*)

  Chiroptes 2 species, bearded saki (*C. satanas*); white-nosed saki (*C. albinasus*)

TITI AND MURIQUI MONKEYS 2 genera, 14 species
  Callicebus 13 species, including yellow-handed titi (*C. torquatus*); masked titi (*C. personatus*); dusky titi (*C. moloch*)

  Brachyteles 1 species, muriqui (*B. arachnoides*)

New World monkeys vary in color. Many species have distinctive patterns, particularly around the head. The nose is broad with widely separated nostrils. Unlike many monkeys, their thumbs cannot grip against the fingers. However, as in other primates, their big toes can be used for gripping. Some species have color vision.

One of the key features of New World monkeys (except the uakaris) is their long, flexible tail. Spider, woolly, and howler monkeys have a fully prehensile tail, which can be curled around objects, such as branches, to grip them. It is also strong enough to hang from, since it can support the whole of the monkey's weight. In contrast, none of the Old World monkeys can hang by their tails alone. The end of the tail has no fur on the underside and is sensitive to touch, just like the tips of fingers. In squirrel monkeys the tail is flexible but not fully prehensile. In capuchins it is not flexible or strong enough for grasping, but is used as a stabilizer.

New World monkeys have two ways of moving. "Swingers" or brachiators, such as spider monkeys, hang in the trees and move hand-over-hand from branch to branch. They have long arms and flexible shoulder joints that allow the arms to swivel in their sockets. In contrast, "leapers," such as squirrel monkeys, have long, powerful legs for launching themselves into the air.

Many of the differences between the species reflect differences in their diets. Spider monkeys are small and energetic, with sharp, narrow teeth. They eat rich, digestible food, mainly fruit and insects. Howler monkeys, on the other hand, are large and specialize in eating leaves. Although leaves are widely available, they are not particularly nutritious. Howler monkeys therefore need big, grinding teeth and a long, modified intestine in which the leaves can be broken down by bacteria. Leaves are easy to find but not rich in energy, so howler monkeys are fairly docile and spend a lot of time resting.

 SEE ALSO Old World Monkey Family, The **4**:40; Marmoset and Tamarin Family, The **4**:86

→ *The unmistakable white facial mask of the male Guianan saki. As in many other New World monkeys, Guianan sakis live in monogamous pairs or small family groups.*

⊕ *A northern night monkey. The night monkey is the only truly nocturnal monkey species. With its enlarged eyes it has excellent night vision.*

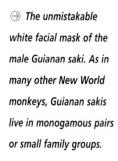

Social Structure

All New World monkeys are sociable to some extent, but the way their groups are arranged is different for each species. Many smaller species, such as titi monkeys, live in family groups of a male and female pair and their immature offspring. Larger monkeys, and also squirrel monkeys, live in bigger groups of two main types. There are "harems," made up of one male and up to three females. There are also groups with many males and females and a definite rank order. Attacks by hawks

and eagles are common, so numerous pairs of eyes are useful to watch for danger. A group can also defend a fruit tree more effectively, and finding food is easier. Brown capuchin monkeys send scouts to search for food. A piercing whistle alerts the other members of the group when a supply is discovered.

About a third of New World monkeys are threatened. Destruction of rain-forest areas is a major problem. In the Amazon Basin many species of woolly and spider monkey are shot for food and in danger of being wiped out.

73

Brown Howler Monkey

Alouatta fusca

Famous for the enormously loud noise it makes, the brown howler monkey is also a specialized leaf eater. It lives in the forests of Brazil.

Common name Brown howler monkey

Scientific name *Alouatta fusca*

Family	Cebidae
Order	Primates
Size	Length head/body: 18–23 in (45–58 cm); tail length: 20–26 in (50–66 cm). Male generally larger than female
Weight	9–16 lb (4–7 kg)
Key features	Chubby, thickset monkey, with swollen throat region in adult males; coat dark reddish brown, paler below
Habits	Tree dwelling; lives in small groups; active mainly during daylight hours
Breeding	Single young born each year after gestation period of about 189 days. Weaned at about 10–12 months; females sexually mature at 3–4 years, males take longer. May live to about 20 years in captivity, 15 in the wild
Voice	Very loud howling and roars made especially by males
Diet	Mainly leaves, but also fruit
Habitat	Tropical forests
Distribution	Coastal forests of southeastern Brazil
Status	Population: unknown, probably low thousands; IUCN Vulnerable; CITES II. Threatened by destruction and fragmentation of forest habitat

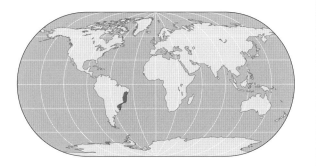

BROWN HOWLER MONKEYS LIVE IN small social groups of a dozen or so individuals. Often, there are two or three adult males, a few females, and younger animals of various ages.

Dawn Chorus

As the sun rises, and before the animals begin their daily routine, the adult males strike up their characteristic howling. The noises they make sometimes include hoarse coughs or low moans, but also spine-chilling roars. The sounds carry for over a mile (1.6 km) through the forests and are a characteristic feature of the jungle in tropical South America. Such special noises are created by forcing air past a bony "voice box" in the throat of the adult males. It is about the size of a golf ball and accounts for the characteristic swollen appearance of the throat in adult males.

It is not entirely clear why howler monkeys make such a noise, but it is probably a means of telling each group where the others are. It is important not to have too many monkeys trying to feed in the same place, and the dawn chorus of howling helps them all keep out of each other's way. It also helps save energy, since the monkeys do not have to chase around looking for intruders or patrol their home range to leave scent marks. If groups of howler monkeys do meet, there is generally a lot of noisy squabbling, charging around, and outright aggression. Such encounters waste energy and are easily avoided by sending out noisy signals. The noises might attract predators, but the monkeys are relatively safe in the treetops.

Howler monkeys are active during the day and move slowly among the tree branches to

feed on leaves. They rarely come to the ground. Even during the day more than half of their time is spent resting. Conserving energy is important because leaves are difficult to digest and not particularly nutritious.

Like other mammals, howler monkeys are unable to digest cellulose, the main chemical material in leaves. Instead, they have microbes in their gut that can break down the material. The monkeys are therefore able to digest the food using a process that is similar to the formation of compost. Colobus monkeys in Africa, which have a similar lifestyle, digest leaves using microbes in their multichambered stomach. The stomach of a howler monkey is more like our own, with a single chamber,

A brown howler monkey feeds on fruit in the Caratinga Reserve, eastern Brazil. A dawn chorus of howls helps warn the monkeys of each other's presence, so that feeding areas do not become overcrowded.

and microbial digestion takes place in enlarged sections of the intestine. The process is not very efficient at the best of times. As a result, howler monkeys are highly selective about what they eat, choosing only the most nutritious leaves. They will also select ripe fruits and flowers whenever they are to hand.

Land of Plenty

The tropical forests have leaves all year round. There are also many different tree species within quite small areas, offering a variety of leaves to eat. Consequently, it is possible for howler monkeys to feed without traveling very far. A single troop of howler monkeys can find all they need in a home range of about 70 to 80 acres (30 ha), and they only need move about a quarter of a mile (400 m) in the course of the day. In contrast, the fruit-eating spider monkeys sometimes have to travel at least 10 times as far to find their food, since ripe fruits are only thinly distributed across the forests.

Howler monkeys are agile animals despite having rather short legs. They have a long prehensile tail, which is naked on the underside and capable of an immensely strong grip: The animal can leap from a tree and arrest its fall by grabbing a branch with just its tail.

There seems to be no distinct breeding season, and young howler monkeys can be born at any time of year. There is only a single baby, and generally at least a year between births. The newborn monkey weighs about 12 ounces (340 g). It holds tightly to its mother's fur and later rides on her back. After about a year weaning is complete, and the young monkey is able to feed itself. Like other slow-breeding mammals, howlers compensate by living to a ripe old age. The average life span is probably about 15 years, although they can live much longer in captivity.

Howler monkeys are threatened by destruction and fragmentation of their forest habitat. At least two isolated local subspecies are considered to be at risk, with populations numbering only about 200 individuals.

Common name
Black- handed spider
monkey (Central
American spider monkey)

Scientific name *Ateles geoffroyi*

Family Cebidae

Order Primates

Size Length head/body: 13–20 in (34–52 cm);
tail length: 24–32 in (60–82 cm)

Weight Male 16–20 lb (7–9 kg);
female 13–20 lb (6–9 kg)

Key features Short, thin fur of various shades of brown,
with black hands and feet; long, slender
limbs and long tail; face often has a mask of
pale skin around the eyes and mouth

Habits Lives in small groups; swings through trees
using hands, feet, and tail; active by day

Breeding Single young born every 2 or 3 years at any
time of year after gestation period of 225
days. Weaned at 1 year; sexually mature at
about 5 years. May live up to 48 years in
captivity, more than 20 in the wild

Voice Barks and screams

Diet Mainly fruit and leaves; also tree bark

Habitat High tree canopy; rarely on the ground

Distribution Central America from Mexico to Panama

Status Population: fairly abundant, probably many
thousands; IUCN Endangered (4 local
subspecies), Vulnerable (3 local subspecies);
CITES I. Still fairly common in some places

Black-Handed Spider Monkey

Ateles geoffroyi

Spider monkeys live up to the classic image of a monkey. They are agile, tree-dwelling creatures that use their tails, hands, and feet to hang from the branches to pluck fruit from the treetops.

SPIDER MONKEYS GET THEIR NAME from the fact that their extraordinarily long limbs and tail, leading from a small body, are somewhat reminiscent of a spider. Unlike the Old World monkeys and many of those living in South America, spider monkeys can hang by their tail. It is long and prehensile. The underside is bare of fur. In fact, it looks like the palm of a hand, being covered with sensitive, creased skin.

Getting Around

Typically, spider monkeys move around by walking along the tops of branches. However, unlike most monkeys, they will also travel rapidly through the trees. They hang below the branches and swing from one to the next, rather like the gibbons of Southeast Asia.

Fruit forms more than three-quarters of their food, although they will also eat flowers, nuts, and occasionally insects or birds' eggs. Sometimes they eat leaves and occasionally nibble at bark—a strange habit, since bark is difficult to digest and not particularly nutritious.

Black-handed spider monkeys prefer tall, mature forests, where the trees offer a continuous canopy of widely spreading limbs. They do not thrive in areas where the forest has been fragmented into small patches. As a result of tree removal, the species is already extinct in some places where it used to occur. Local subspecies have developed in some areas, but they are confined to small patches of forest due to clearance of trees for timber and agriculture.

⊙ *Spider monkeys normally grip the branches with at least two feet as well as the tail, which they use as a fifth limb. One or more of the hands is then left free to pick the fruit on which they feed.*

 SEE ALSO Gibbon Family, The **4**:36; Monkey, Brown Howler **4**:74; Monkey, Humboldt's Woolly **4**:82

in a mango tree full of ripe fruits, for example, larger numbers sometimes gather.

Catnapping

Black-handed spider monkeys are generally active in the highest part of the tree canopy. They are only active during the day—especially early in the morning and late afternoon—but spend much of the time resting. They often sprawl along a branch with their arms and legs dangling down each side. They are difficult to see; but if disturbed by a human or a predator, they will stand on the branch, stamping their feet and shaking the vegetation. Sometimes they break off small branches and throw them, growling in a menacing fashion.

Spider monkeys do not travel far and usually range over no more than about 1 square mile (1.6 sq. km). Females, especially those with young, will restrict their activity to a small core area. Males help each other defend their group territory from strangers.

Spider monkey numbers do not increase rapidly since they produce only one young at a time, with at least two or three years between births. Like other slow-breeding mammals, black-handed spider monkeys compensate for producing few young by living a long time.

They now survive in critically small numbers. Elsewhere, black-handed spider monkeys are sometimes fairly numerous, but they are often shot for food. They may also be prone to yellow fever, a disease transmitted by mosquitoes.

Spider monkeys live in Central America, where the climate is usually warm and moist. The type of tropical forest that grows there supports a huge variety of trees, so at least some will be producing fruit at all times of the year. The monkeys normally live in groups of about 20, although they split up into smaller foraging parties to avoid competing with each other for food. Where there is plenty to eat, as

Common name Squirrel monkey (common squirrel monkey)

Scientific name *Saimiri sciureus*

Family Cebidae

Order Primates

Size Length head/body: 11–14.5 in (28–37 cm); tail length: 14.5–18 in (37–45 cm)

Weight 19–44 oz (550–1,250 g)

Key features Small olive-green monkey with orange hands and white around the face; muzzle black

Habits Active by day in groups of 30–40 animals

Breeding Single young born once a year after gestation period of 170 days. Weaned at about 1 year; females sexually mature at 3 years, males at 5 years. May live up to 30 years in captivity, probably fewer in the wild

Voice Variety of squeaks, chirps, and purring noises

Diet Mainly fruit and insects

Habitat Forests, including mangroves from sea level to 6,500 ft (2,000 m)

Distribution Tropical South America

Status Population: abundant; CITES II. Common animal. Large numbers previously captured for the pet trade, now protected in the wild and no longer threatened by such activities

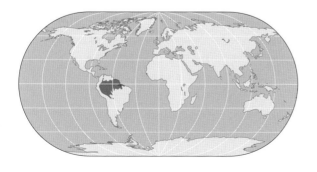

Squirrel Monkey

Saimiri sciureus

The small, greenish squirrel monkey has been widely collected for the pet trade, but remains fairly common over a large part of tropical South America.

THERE ARE FOUR OR FIVE SPECIES of squirrel monkeys, each occupying a different region of South and Central America. The common squirrel monkey is found almost throughout a huge area of tropical forest. It ranges from Venezuela to southern Brazil and westward into the foothills of the Andes mountains in Colombia. All squirrel monkeys have short, dense fur that is brightly colored, in contrast to the drab browns of most monkeys. They appear greenish, with a white face and neatly contrasting black muzzle. The underside is yellow, and the feet are orange. Squirrel monkeys are not only attractive in appearance, they are also cute in their behavior. They are active, sociable creatures, constantly interacting with each other. They communicate using a wide range of sounds, almost as if they were having a conversation.

The Perfect Pet

The squirrel monkey's endearing features, coupled with a conveniently small size, made it extremely popular in zoos and as a household pet. The animals are easy to keep in captivity, where they may live for up to 30 years. As a result of their appealing characteristics, large numbers were captured and exported for the pet trade. It is estimated that more than 173,000 were imported into the United States alone between 1968 and 1972. About half went into zoos or became household pets, while the rest were used for medical research. Trade in squirrel monkeys, and the consequent pressure on wild populations, has now been brought under control. In the wild the squirrel

⊖ *A common squirrel monkey feeds in the forests of Ecuador. Fruit and insects are its preferred food, but it will also eat other animal material, flowers, and nuts.*

groups may subdivide into small foraging parties during the day, but gather together again from time to time. During their daytime activities they often stop and take a rest before continuing to forage. Squirrel monkeys are active mostly in the trees, but they will occasionally come to the ground. Each group ranges through about 40 to 50 acres (16 to 20 ha). Within the group's communal home range a small core area will be used by that group alone, although the outer regions may be shared with other squirrel monkeys. In good habitat there can be over 250 squirrel monkeys living in 1 square mile of forest (100 per sq. km).

Repertoire of Calls

The animals keep in touch with each other using a wider range of vocalizations than other monkeys. They squeak, squawk, and purr. They also make barking noises and may scream with pain during fighting. Altogether, they seem to have at least 20 different recognizable calls. It is a helpful way of keeping in touch for an animal that lives in dense foliage, with members of the group widely scattered. It is also a substitute for using scent as a means of communication.

In the wild squirrel monkeys seem to breed at any time of the year, although births often occur in one season. Each newborn squirrel monkey weighs about 3 to 4 ounces (100 g). The babies cling to their mother's fur for a few weeks, then ride on her back. However, they do not become independent until they are about a year old. Although the adult males fight fiercely to mate with the females, they play no part in raising the young. Indeed, males may be driven away by the mothers, who prefer to look after their offspring without help.

monkey now has little to fear from humans. It is too small to be much use for food, its skin has no value, and its forest habitat remains largely intact. Moreover, squirrel monkeys, unlike many other species, are able to survive in fragmented habitats and also among the new growth and planted trees that often replace natural forests. However, the continued expansion of cattle rearing in South America, which results in conversion of large areas of forest to grassland, threatens squirrel monkeys just as it does every other tree-dwelling animal.

Common squirrel monkeys live in humid lowland forests, where they form larger social groups than any other species of South American monkey. Groups of up to 300 have been reported, although it is more normal to find between 30 and 50 living together. Larger

Common name Red uakari
(bald uakari, white
uakari)

Scientific name *Cacajao calvus*

Family Cebidae

Order Primates

Size Length head/body: 21–22 in (54–57 cm); tail
length: 5.5–7.3 in (14–18.5 cm)

Weight Male 7.6 lb (3.4 kg); female 6.4 lb (2.9 kg)

Key features Small monkey with long, coarse, pale-
brown fur and bare, red face; tail very short

Habits Tree dwelling, but often descends to the
ground; lives in social groups numbering
15–30 animals; active by day

Breeding One young born every 2 years or so after
gestation period of about 6 months. Weaned
at 20 months; females sexually mature at 3
years, males at 5 years. May live over 30
years in captivity, 10 in the wild

Voice Generally silent, except during noisy fights

Diet Mostly seeds, but also flowers, fruit, leaves,
and insects

Habitat Wet lowland forests

Distribution Upper Amazon into eastern Peru and
southern Colombia

Status Population: unknown, probably many
thousands; IUCN Endangered (3 local
subspecies); Vulnerable (1 subspecies);
CITES I. Fairly common, but threatened by
hunting and forest clearance; certain
subspecies are rare

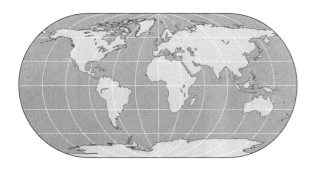

Red Uakari

Cacajao calvus

*The bald, blushing face of the red
uakari is highly distinctive and sets
it apart from other mammals of the
South American jungles.*

ALTHOUGH IT IS FOUND OVER a wide geographical
area, the red uakari is rather more specific in its
habitat than most South American primates. It
is found mostly in the trees that fringe small
rivers and lakes deep in the forest. It is
particularly associated with the so-called "black-
water" rivers whose water resembles tea
without milk owing to the large amounts of
natural peaty plant chemicals in the water.

Avoiding the Floods

Red uakaris live in the tops of the largest trees
and tend to stay there, particularly during the
wet season when the forest floor is flooded. In
many parts of the upper Amazon flood waters
cover the forest floor to a depth of 6.5 feet
(often 2 m or more) for several weeks of the
year. The flooded forests are the main home of
the red uakari. The common species is found
from Colombia and Peru into Brazil. A second
species, the black-headed uakari, lives in
Venezuela and adjacent parts of northern Brazil.

The red uakari is the only South American
monkey with a short tail. It has a red face, as if
blushing. Otherwise, it is rather expressionless.
In captivity the face tends to bleach to a white
or yellowish color. The red uakari's bald head
and large, fleshy ears are almost like those of a
human, but there is little fat under the skin,
especially in adult males. As a result, the
angular parts of the skull and bulging jaw
muscles tend to show through, making the face
look rather corpselike. Uakaris from different
parts of the species' range differ in their general
coloration and are often classified as different
subspecies. One is nearly white, while others are

① A white uakari travels through the lower part of the Amazonian rainforest canopy. The white form is sometimes considered to be a separate subspecies.

yellowish. Another typical form has shaggy, rusty red fur. Uakaris can leap 20 feet (6 m or more), but seem not to spring from branch to branch as much as other monkeys do. Nor do they swing by their arms or tail. Instead, they run and scamper on all fours along the thick branches of the lower canopy, returning to the topmost branches to feed.

Foraging in the Treetops

Uakaris are normally active during the day. They feed mostly on fruit, probably assisted by their forward-pointing lower incisor teeth. Saki monkeys, close relatives of uakaris, share the same arrangement of teeth. Uakaris also eat a lot of seeds and sometimes leaves and small animals, including insects. They have extremely supple and sensitive hands. They grip their food with the whole hand or between the fingers,

but do not use the thumb the way we do. They move around in the treetops in small groups of up to 30 animals. However, larger groupings have been reported containing as many as 100 animals. In captivity uakaris will squabble to establish dominance. It is likely that a similar process occurs in the wild, creating a social hierarchy within the group.

Females are able to breed at about three years old and can continue to produce young until they are at least 10 years of age. The mother nurses her baby for nearly two years and will not have another offspring until the nursing period is over. Like many other primates, the slow rate of reproduction is offset by living a long time. Uakaris can live to be at least 10 years old, perhaps considerably more, and one is said to have lived at least 31 years in captivity. However, populations are unable to respond rapidly to compensate for losses due to hunting or accidents. Some localized subspecies of uakari have been reduced to low numbers and are now threatened with extinction.

In some areas uakaris have become scarce at the hands of the pet trade. Traditionally, the animals were shot with a blowgun dart tipped with a dilute dose of poison. The uakari would be caught when it fell from the branches and revived later. Excessive hunting has also taken a heavy toll in some areas, while forest clearance to supply the timber industry is another threat. Removing the trees not only takes away habitat and food sources, but creates large open spaces between the remaining populations. As a result, groups are prevented from mixing freely and so run the risk of inbreeding.

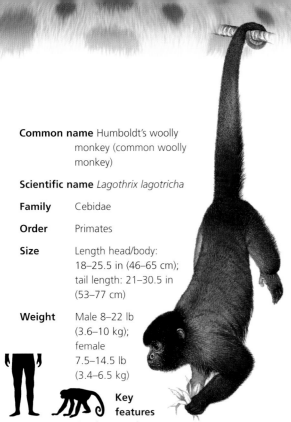

Common name Humboldt's woolly
monkey (common woolly
monkey)

Scientific name *Lagothrix lagotricha*

Family	Cebidae
Order	Primates
Size	Length head/body: 18–25.5 in (46–65 cm); tail length: 21–30.5 in (53–77 cm)
Weight	Male 8–22 lb (3.6–10 kg); female 7.5–14.5 lb (3.4–6.5 kg)

**Key
features**
Fur dense and
moderately long; body gray to olive-brown or
dark brown; the rounded head is often
darker, almost black; strong prehensile tail

Habits	Diurnal; prefers to stay high up in tree canopy; lives in mixed-sex groups of 20–70
Breeding	Single baby born every 1.5–3 years after gestation period of 223 days. Weaned at 9–12 months; sexually mature at 6–8 years. May live 24 years in captivity, 10 in the wild
Voice	Range of yelps, screams, chuckles, and barks
Diet	Fruit; also leaves and other vegetable material
Habitat	Mature, undisturbed rain forest from sea level to 9,850 ft (3,000 m)
Distribution	Bolivia, Brazil, Colombia, Ecuador, Peru, and Venezuela
Status	Population: probably many thousands; IUCN Critically Endangered (1 subspecies); Vulnerable (2 subspecies); CITES II. Relatively abundant, not considered to be at risk

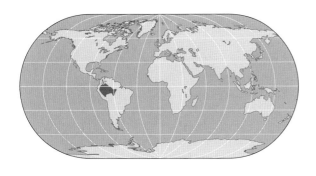

Humboldt's Woolly Monkey

Lagothrix lagotricha

Humboldt's woolly monkey is a large, stocky animal that forages for fruit high in the canopy of undisturbed rain forests. Its dense, woolly fur can be a wide range of colors from smoky gray to black.

THE HUMBOLDT'S OR COMMON woolly monkey is one of the largest monkeys in South America. Despite its relatively heavy build, it is agile in the trees, using its prehensile tail as a fifth limb. The tail has a bare patch on the underside at the tip, with a ridged texture that is highly sensitive and gives a good grip. The rest of the tail is strong and muscular, and can easily support the monkey's hanging weight. The woolly monkey's hands and feet are also good at grasping: Its fingers and toes are well developed, and each has a long, pointed nail.

Woolly by Name

The woolly monkey's thick coat with its lining of dense underfur gives the species its name. Its coat sets it apart from many other monkeys, on whom the fur is often quite sparse. The woolly monkey's color varies from smoky or blue-gray, olive-brown, tawny, dark brown, or even black. Some individuals may be a yellowish buff color.

Woolly monkeys are mainly fruit eaters, preferring soft, ripe fruit such as figs. They can excrete the seeds a long distance away from the parent tree and so are an important agent in seed dispersal. When ripe fruit is not in season, woolly monkeys will feed on seeds, flowers, and leaves. They also eat insects such as ants and termites. In captivity they have been seen catching sparrows that fly into their cage.

Woolly monkeys forage high in the jungle canopy, often in the tops of the emergent trees that grow out above the rest of the forest. They also sometimes descend to the shrub layer to feed. In the wild they rarely need to come down to ground level; while in captivity, they walk

⊝ A mother with her young. When females reach sexual maturity, they usually leave the group in which they were born, while males tend to stay.

easily on the ground, often on two legs. They are reluctant leapers, preferring instead to move around gaps in the canopy.

Flexible Social Groups

Woolly monkeys live in loose social groups of 20 to 70 animals (30 to 40 is most common). Within the group there are roughly equal numbers of males and females. Although males form a hierarchy based on age and strength, the top-ranking males do not command sole mating rights with their females. In a large group a receptive female usually mates many times with several males in the group, but most often with the lead male. In a smaller group, without the distraction of other females the lead male may monopolize a receptive female and prevent other males from mating with her.

Group membership is flexible, with animals sometimes leaving to join other groups. Subadult females are the most common wanderers and may spend hours or days with other groups. Groups of woolly monkeys will often consort with other monkey species, such as howlers or capuchin monkeys. The other species do not compete for the same food, and grouping together means there are more pairs of eyes to watch for predators.

Each group of woolly monkeys has a home range of about 1.5 to 4 square miles (4 to 10 sq. km). The boundaries are not enforced, and the ranges usually overlap with those of other groups. However, a group may sometimes temporarily defend areas such as favorite fruiting trees. Animals, particularly the males, leave scent marks by wetting a surface with saliva, then rubbing their chest on it.

Woolly monkeys are vulnerable to human encroachment, since they cannot adapt to secondary forests that replace mature forests when they are felled. In addition, young woolly monkeys are often sold as pets; it is estimated that for every baby that makes it to market alive, 10 will be killed or die in transit. Woolly monkeys are also hunted for food, since their large size makes them profitable targets.

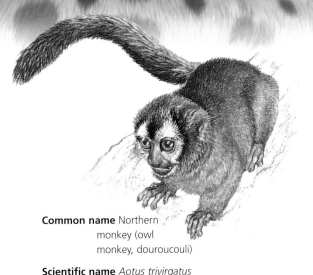

Common name Northern
 monkey (owl
 monkey, douroucouli)

Scientific name *Aotus trivirgatus*

Family   Cebidae

Order   Primates

Size   Length head/body: 12–16.5 in (30–42 cm);
             tail length: 10–17 in (25–43 cm)

Weight 1.8–2.8 lb (0.8–1.3 kg)

Key features Grizzled brown or gray on back,
             limbs, and back of head; underside buff-
             white; head has triangular white patches
             above large eyes; 3 black stripes run between
             and either side of eyes, converging on top of
             head

Habits   Nocturnal; arboreal: mainly in top half of
             forest canopy; lives in family groups of 2–5

Breeding Usually only a single offspring born at any
             time of year after gestation period of
             120–133 days. Weaned at 6–8 months;
             sexually mature at 3 years. May live about 27
             years in captivity, 10–15 in the wild

Voice   Wide variety of calls, including shrill cries,
             hoots, grunts, clicks, and squeaks

Diet   Small fruit; also leaves, nectar, plant gums,
             and insects; for extra protein eggs and small
             animals, such as lizards and frogs

Habitat Primary and secondary forests from sea level
             to 10,500 ft (3,200 m)

Distribution Tropical Central and South America:
             Panama, Brazil, Venezuela, and Peru

Status   Population: probably low thousands; CITES II.
             Widespread and fairly abundant

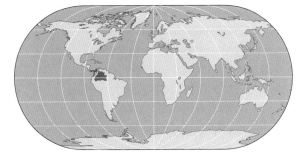

Northern Night Monkey

Aotus trivirgatus

*Night monkeys are the only truly nocturnal monkey.
They sleep during the day and forage for fruit at night.*

NORTHERN NIGHT MONKEYS ARE diminutive creatures.
They are the smallest members of the South
American monkey family (Cebidae) and the
world's only nocturnal monkey. Their large,
brown eyes set in a white face give them an
owlish appearance, hence their alternative
common name of owl monkey. Their unusual
way of life helps them avoid predators and
competition. As a result, the northern night
monkey is highly successful. This species and its
close relatives now live throughout most of
tropical South America.

Night Vision

Night monkeys begin activity about 15 minutes
after sunset and retreat to a safe place—in a
tree hollow or tangle of climbing vines—at
dawn. Their large eyes provide excellent night
vision, but the animals always need some light
to see by. On moonless or cloudy nights they
travel shorter distances and are most active at
dawn and dusk. On bright, moonlit nights,
however, they move confidently through the
trees, making daring leaps of 10 to 16 feet
(3 to 5 m) and balancing along thin vines. Their
agility is due partly to their small size. Also, their
fingers are long and narrow, with expanded
pads at the tips to provide extra grip. Unlike in
many other South American monkeys, the long,
black-tipped tail is not prehensile, so the
animals cannot use it to hang by or to grip
branches. Instead, the tail is used for balancing,
more like that of a squirrel. Night monkeys also
have thick fur that is denser than in most other
South American monkeys. Its purpose is to
protect the animal against nighttime chills.

Night monkeys venture out when all other
monkeys and most predators have gone to
roost. Being nocturnal, they can hide from birds

of prey—the most serious predators of small monkeys, but which are only active by day. There are nocturnal predators, such as jaguars and ocelots, but they are too big and heavy to catch night monkeys in the trees. The night monkeys also avoid competition with the larger daytime monkeys, such as capuchins, who would chase them away from fruit trees.

Evidence suggests that night monkeys evolved from day-active monkeys, since they still have color vision (which is not needed at nighttime). Also, their eyes do not have a

⊕ Night monkeys tend to travel quietly and relatively slowly, often staying in a single fruit tree for hours at a time.

tapetum lucidum—the light-reflective layer present in most nocturnal animals.

Night monkeys live in close family units of two to five individuals—an adult pair and their young of up to three years old.

Demanding Babies

Adults pair for life and produce on average one baby a year. Mating and births can occur at any time of year, but births peak in the fruit-ripening season. The one baby is relatively large at birth and grows quickly. It takes the concerted effort of both parents to nurture it. For the first four months the father carries and cares for the baby for most of the time, returning it to the mother every two or three hours for suckling. Older siblings also take a turn in childcare duties. At about three years young night monkeys leave their family group to search for their own partner and territory.

Each family group guards a territory of about 22 acres (9 ha). The boundaries are defended against other monkeys with aggressive displays of whooping, stiff-legged jumping, and chases. Such displays can end in wrestling matches, but usually last less than 10 minutes, with the trespasser retreating.

Night monkeys communicate by using sound and smell. Individuals sniff each other when they meet. They urinate on their hands, then rub them on a branch to communicate sexual attraction. Unlike most other monkeys, social grooming is rare and only used during mating. When threatened, night monkeys sound the alarm with a "wook wook." The cry is amplified by a throat pouch like a smaller version of the howler monkey's.

Northern night monkeys are tolerant of disturbance and often live near humans. They can survive in many habitat types as long as there are some trees. However, they still suffer when areas are deforested for building development or cattle ranches. The monkeys are also killed for their meat and fur, and collected as pets and for use in experiments.

The Marmoset and Tamarin Family

Marmosets and tamarins live in Central and South America. The Amazon Basin is home to most of the species, but some occur as far north as Costa Rica in Central America. A few species in Paraguay and Bolivia live in patches of trees dotted among the savanna, but most prefer dense rain forest.

Marmosets and tamarins have many features that make them unique among primates. Instead of nails, they have claws on all fingers and toes, except the big toe. They have two molar teeth on each side of their upper and lower jaws instead of the three found in other primates. They live in social groups in which one female is dominant. She gives birth to twins, which is rare in primates. All members of the group help rear the young.

The hair of marmosets and tamarins is usually fine and silky. It comes in a range of colors, including black, white, and golden-yellow. In some individuals single hairs are banded in two or more colors. Most species have some form of fancy adornment, such as a crest, fringe, mustache, or ear tufts. The cotton-top tamarin of Colombia has a pure-white crest that cascades to its shoulders, and the lion tamarins are so called because of the large mane of hair around their neck and shoulders. All tamarins have a tail, but it cannot grip branches, unlike that of many typical South American monkeys.

Tamarins and marmosets are among the smallest of all primates. The pygmy marmoset is the tiniest and fits easily into the palm of a human hand.

Habits and Diet

Marmosets and tamarins are active during the day. At night they shelter in crevices and holes in trees, often those made by woodpeckers. They are agile creatures, with fast, jerky movements that make them look nervous and highly strung. They will run along horizontal branches and leap from tree to tree, but do not swing from branches using their tail or hands.

Tamarins and marmosets eat a variety of animals, including insects. They are especially fond of grasshoppers, beetles, and stick insects. They also prey on spiders, snails, frogs, lizards, and small snakes. They will eat plants, taking young buds and flowers, but not leaves. Fruit is a favored food, and the animals select small, sweet, ripe examples from among the many available. The seeds and pips are often swallowed, to be dropped elsewhere among their feces. Marmosets and tamarins are therefore important agents for dispersing seeds within the forest. Most species will also eat tree gum. Where the bark of trees is damaged, by insects, for example, the tree exudes a sticky sap to close the hole and stop infection. Marmosets—especially the pygmy marmoset—have specialized in using it. They gouge their own holes in trees, using specially modified lower teeth.

Family Callitrichidae: 6 genera, 38 species

MARMOSETS 3 genera, 18 species

Callithrix 6 species, including Geoffroy's marmoset (*C. geoffroyi*); common marmoset (*C. jacchus*)

Cebuella 1 species, pygmy marmoset (*C. (Callithrix) pygmaea*)

Mico 11 species, including silvery marmoset (*M. (Callithrix) argentata*); dwarf marmoset (*M. (Callithrix) humilis*)

TAMARINS 1 genus, 15 species

Saguinus includes saddleback tamarin (*S. fusciollis*); emperor tamarin (*S. imperator*); cotton-top tamarin (*S. oedipus*)

LION TAMARINS 1 genus, 4 species

Leontopithecus includes golden lion tamarin (*L. rosalia*); black lion tamarin (*L. chrysopygus*)

GOELDI'S MONKEY 1 genus, 1 species

Callimico (*C. goeldii*)

 SEE ALSO New World Monkey Family, The **4:**72; Tamarin, Golden Lion **4:**88; Marmoset, Common **4:**92

← Geoffroy's marmoset from northwestern Colombia, Panama, and Costa Rica combines a monkey's face with an almost catlike body.

Threats

Habitat destruction, particularly in the Amazon rain forests where most of the species live, is threatening the survival of all tamarins and marmosets. Those most at risk are species that live in one small area. The golden lion tamarin, for example, occurs only in what is left of the coastal forest of Brazil. Over the years it has become one of the world's most threatened mammals.

In the recent past many tamarins and marmosets were caught for the pet trade. Others were captured for zoos or laboratory research, putting yet more pressure on the already shrinking populations. The problem of animals being taken from the wild is now largely controlled, since international agreements between countries are in place to monitor trade in rare animals. Many species are also breeding well in captivity, thereby reducing the need to take animals from the wild. Captive breeding is also allowing the reintroduction of some species to areas from which they have been lost.

Social Life and Defense of Territory

Tamarins and marmosets live in small groups of up to 20 individuals. Within groups there is little aggression, unlike in other primates, among whom males are constantly competing for dominance. Each social group has a single dominant female who mates with a number of males in the group. The dominant female prevents other females from breeding by her behavior and by chemical signals (pheromones) in her scent marks. She gives birth to twins—usually once a year for tamarins, but twice a year in marmosets. The males assist in the birth by licking the newborn infant clean. They carry the babies most of the time, returning them to the female for feeding every two or three hours. When the infants start eating soft food, all members of the group help feed them.

Each group defends its own home range with smells and loud calls. Marmosets use scent marking to define their territories and to communicate with other members of the group. Some will urinate in the tree holes that they have gouged. Other animals feeding on the tree sap will smell the scent of the hole's original owner.

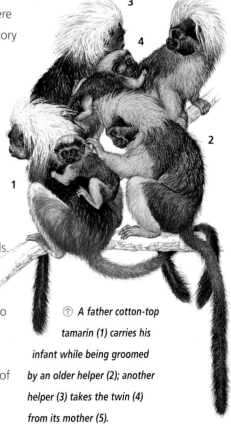

↑ A father cotton-top tamarin (1) carries his infant while being groomed by an older helper (2); another helper (3) takes the twin (4) from its mother (5).

Common name Golden lion tamarin

Scientific name *Leontopithecus rosalia*

Family Callitrichidae

Order Primates

Size Length head/body: 8–13 in (20–31 cm); tail length: 12.5–16 in (32–40 cm)

Weight 21–28 oz (600–800 g)

Key features Small, lively monkey with a long, silky golden coat; long hair on crown, cheeks, and sides of neck forms mane; long tail; bare, flattened face with widely spaced nostrils

Habits Social animal that lives in small groups of 3–7 individuals; active during the day, spending most of the time in the dense middle layers of the forest; rests at night in tree holes

Breeding Young (most commonly twins) born September–March after gestation period of 128 days. Weaned at 12 weeks; sexually mature at 2–3 years. May live 28 years in captivity, many fewer in the wild

Voice A variety of calls, including trills, clucks, and whines

Diet Mostly fruit and insects; small animals such as frogs and lizards; also birds' eggs

Habitat Lowland tropical forests from sea level to about 3,000 ft (1,000 m)

Distribution Rio de Janeiro state, southeastern Brazil

Status Population: fewer than 1,000; IUCN Critically Endangered; CITES I. Destruction of lowland forest is greatest threat to survival

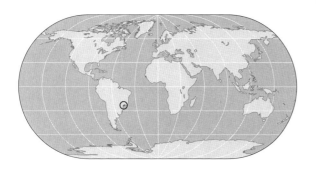

Golden Lion Tamarin

Leontopithecus rosalia

The golden lion tamarin is one of the most threatened mammals in the world. It has been rescued from the brink of extinction by successful reintroduction of captive-bred animals to their natural habitat.

LION TAMARINS ARE ONLY THE size of squirrels, but they are still the largest members of the callitrichid family. There are four types of lion tamarin, all of which are threatened in the wild. The four species have a golden coloration, but only the golden lion tamarin is golden over its entire body. The others are the black-faced lion tamarin (*Leontopithecus caissara*), golden-headed lion tamarin (*L. chrysomelas*), and black lion tamarin (*L. chrysopygus*).

Golden Fur

The golden lion tamarin is almost uniformly a golden-red color, with the occasional splash of orange, brown, or black on the tail and hands. It has soft, silky fur and a thick golden mane of long hairs on the top of the head, cheeks, throat, and neck. Its stunning color is one of the reasons that the animal is now so close to extinction. Demand for the golden lion tamarin as a pet and zoo animal has meant that many have been taken from the wild. However, by far the largest threat has been the destruction of the lowland forests in which it lives.

Like other tamarins, golden lions are diurnal. At night they sleep in tree holes or occasionally among vines or dense creepers that grow on tree branches. Tree holes provide a warm, safe shelter for the night. They must be at least 4 inches (10 cm) in diameter, but not so large that predators can get in.

Tamarins spend most of their time in trees at a height of 10 to 33 feet (3 to 10 m). Here the dense canopy of leaves protects them from the sharp eyes of hawks and other raptors. The tangle of vines and branches provide easy

type of call for large birds flying overhead: When other tamarins hear it, they head for the shelter of the tree trunks or sometimes just drop to the ground.

Family Groups

Golden lion tamarins are social animals, living in groups of between two and 11 animals, although five or six is most common. The group usually consists of a mating pair of adults, plus the juvenile offspring from one or two recent litters. Sometimes extended family members are included. Some groups contain two adult males. However, only the dominant one will father the female's offspring, by monopolizing her at the time when she is likely to conceive. Groups with more than one adult female are infrequent; but when it happens, it is usually only the dominant female that breeds. Her aggression prevents subordinate females from mating, but in times of plenty the second female may also breed. Unlike most other tamarins and marmosets, the dominant female does not seem to exert any pheromone control (chemical signals) over her subordinates to prevent them from breeding.

Groups can travel 0.8 to 1.6 miles (1.3 to 2.6 km) a day when foraging. They occupy home ranges of up to 500 acres (200 ha), although the average is nearer 100 acres (40 ha). Golden lion tamarins are territorial and will defend the core of their home range against other groups. They use scent markings from the neck and genital region, and threat calls and postures. Aggressive postures include staring with an open mouth and arching their back. Chases sometimes end in fights.

⊕ *The golden lion tamarin's magnificent coat made it one of the most highly sought after animals in zoos and by private owners. It is now illegal to take specimens from the wild.*

pathways between trees, so the animals rarely have to use the ground for getting from one to another. Golden lion tamarins are very agile and leap from branch to branch with ease, using all four limbs. They dart around quickly and nervously, constantly on the move.

Golden lion tamarins are mainly killed by hawks and other raptors, as well as cats and large snakes. Recently a weasel-like animal called the tayra has learned to dig tamarins from their nest holes and is wiping out whole groups in some areas. Tamarins use alarm calls when they feel threatened. They have a specific

The lion tamarin's diet consists mostly of fruit and insects, but it also eats spiders, snails, frogs, small lizards, and birds. It consumes eggs, plant gums, and nectar when available. It uses its long, slender hands and fingers to probe for prey in the crevices of tree bark, rotting wood, piles of dead leaves, or dense foliage.

A Family Affair

Rearing young is a family effort. All members cooperate, but the father does most of the work. The female gives birth in the warmest and wettest period of the year, between September and March. In captivity seasonality of birth can be broken so that a female can have two litters per year. Unlike most other primates, lion tamarins usually have twins rather than a single young. The babies are born fully furred, and their eyes can open immediately. For the first few weeks they cling tightly to their mother, but the father soon takes over in carrying the young around. By the third week he spends more time with them than the mother. Other members of the group also help with rearing. It is a valuable learning experience for juveniles who may have their own young in a year or two's time.

At about five weeks the young get more adventurous, leaving the safety of their parent's fur to explore their surroundings. They are weaned at around 90 days. Sometimes groups share food by offering it to the young family members. At other times the juveniles playfully steal it, which is tolerated by their elders. Young animals will often make a rasping noise as they try to take food from another animal.

Females reach sexual maturity at 18 months and males at 24 months. Unlike most other primates, it is the young females that are likely to leave their family group first. When they become mature, young females are chased away by their mother. They often have a hard time finding a new territory and are chased aggressively by members of established groups until they find an unoccupied area.

Disappearing Forest

The golden lion tamarin lives in the narrow strip of Atlantic coastal forest in eastern Brazil. It was the first part of Brazil to be colonized by Europeans and is now the most heavily populated region in the country. The lowland forest is easy to get to and easy to clear. For well over two centuries trees have been felled for timber and to make charcoal or cleared to make way for plantations, rice fields, cattle pasture, buildings, and roads. At one time the habitat in which the tamarins lived covered an area about the size of Texas. Now only 2 percent remains as forest. Even worse, much of the area is divided into tiny fragments of forest separated by open ground, so groups of animals cannot mix. As a result, inbreeding is a problem among the remaining tamarins.

A coordinated captive-breeding program began in 1973, involving zoos in many countries. At that time golden lion tamarins were on the brink of extinction. There were only about 200 animals left in the wild and 70 in zoos. Within 10 years the numbers of captive animals had increased to 600, providing enough to start reintroducing them to the Brazilian forest.

Zoo-bred animals were released into a nature reserve near Rio de Janeiro. At first many of the released animals died. Some were killed by predators, partly because they spent more time on the ground than the more wary wild

Tamarins and Bromeliads

Bromeliads are a common sight in the humid forests where the tamarins live. They are plants that grow high on the branches of other trees without ever touching the soil.

Many of the insects on which the tamarins feed hide in the bromeliads' leaves. In the center of each bromeliad plant is a hollow that collects rainwater. The wells are useful sources of drinking water for tamarins, and they also harbor another of the tamarin's favorite foods—small frogs.

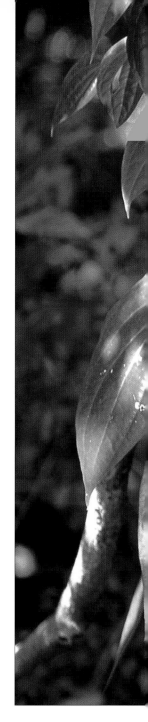

⬆ *Golden lion tamarins tend to inhabit the dense branches and vines that grow at heights of 10 to 33 feet (3 to 10 m) in the forest canopy. Here they are safe from the sharp eyes of hawks and other birds of prey.*

⊕ *The golden-headed lion tamarin is one of four species of lion tamarin, all of which are threatened. Its home in the Una Biological Reserve in Brazil is being stripped of trees by landless squatters.*

animals normally do. Also, they were not used to finding their own food, so they relied on handouts. As scientists and zookeepers became better at preparing captive-bred animals for life in the wild, survival levels increased. Now reintroduced animals have a better breeding rate than those kept in zoos.

Because each family group needs an area of about 100 acres (40 ha), patches of forest that are any smaller will not be enough to support the lion tamarins and allow their offspring to spread. An important part of the conservation program has been to plant more trees in deforested areas in order to create corridors that link small patches of habitat. A huge tree-planting program to improve the area for lion tamarins has also benefited many other forest animals. Another vital aspect of the conservation program has been educating local people. By encouraging people, especially ranch owners, to value the animals, it is more likely that they will want to protect the forest. Brazilians are now proud of their tamarins.

Common Marmoset

Callithrix jacchus

Common marmosets are very adaptable and live in many types of forest. Because they are small and easy to keep in captivity, many have been used in biomedical research.

Common name Common marmoset

Scientific name *Callithrix jacchus*

Family Callitrichidae

Order Primates

Size Length head/body: 4.7–6 in (12–15 cm); tail length: 12–14 in (30–35 cm)

Weight 10.5–12.7 oz (300–360 g)

Key features Mottled gray-brown coat; crown blackish with a white patch on forehead; long white ear tufts; gray and white banded tail

Habits Active during the day; lives in stable groups of up to 15 animals

Breeding One to 4 young (commonly twins) born twice yearly after gestation period of 130–150 days. Weaned at 100 days; males sexually mature at 11–15 months, females at 14–24 months. May live 16 years in captivity, 10 in the wild

Voice Soft "phee" contact call; angry chatter and high-pitched whistle as a warning call

Diet Tree sap, insects, spiders, fruit, flowers, and nectar; also lizards, frogs, eggs, and nestlings

Habitat Atlantic coast forest and gallery forest along rivers; forest patches in dry thorn scrub and bush savanna

Distribution Northeastern Brazil west and south from the Rio Parnaiba

Status Population: abundant; CITES I. Relatively common and widespread; not seriously threatened

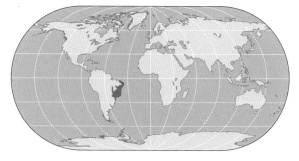

COMMON MARMOSETS ARE SMALL, lively animals with dark and light bands around the tail, long ear tufts, and a white blaze on the forehead. The rest of the head is usually dark brown, and the back is a grayish brown with faint horizontal stripes. The infants lack ear tufts and have gray fur on their head and neck. By the time they are juveniles, the characteristic striped markings have grown through.

Easy Going

Common marmosets originally came from the forests of northeastern Brazil. However, they are highly adaptable animals and are now thriving in many other areas where they have been introduced. They even live in the suburbs of Buenos Aires, Argentina. They are flexible about the type of forest they live in and can use dense riverside trees, dry scrub, and even parks and plantations. Most habitats are suitable, as long as there are enough trees producing sap or gum and hiding places from predators. The common marmoset's flexibility means that it is less threatened by habitat loss than many of the more specialized tamarins.

Like other related species, common marmosets are active during the day. They live in stable groups of up to 15 individuals (most normally eight to 10). Each group has a home range of approximately 25 to 100 acres (10 to 40 ha). The group visits about a third of its total range each day, traveling up to 1.2 miles (2 km) in search of food.

Common marmosets defend their territories from rival groups with a loud "phee" call and perform a display in which they raise their tails,

⊕ *Common marmosets are active during the day. Tree saps are the most important part of their diet, and the animals spend up to 70 percent of their foraging time feeding on them.*

Common marmosets also eat insects, including grasshoppers, cicadas, crickets, and cockroaches. When tackling a large insect, a marmoset will pounce, grab it with both hands, bite off its head, and eat the rest, leaving just the wings and intestines. Common marmosets will often follow swarming army ants, catching the insects that they disturb on the forest floor.

In a group there is usually one dominant breeding female, one or two dominant males, and their offspring. There may also be one or two unrelated immigrants. Smelly hormones (called pheromones) produced by the dominant female prevent younger but sexually mature females from breeding. The hormones, which affect behavior and physiology, also help avoid inbreeding. A restriction in the number of breeding females means there are always plenty of young, nonbreeding females around to provide help when the dominant female has babies. By enlisting the help of group members to raise the young, common marmosets are able to breed successfully twice a year.

During the gestation period the pregnant mother needs to eat voraciously, since together twins can equal up to 40 percent of her own body weight. The babies are completely dependent on their carers for their first two weeks. They are usually carried around by the males, who return them to their mother for feeding. By the age of two months they can travel on their own and spend much time play fighting and learning to catch insects. They begin to reach breeding condition at about 12 to 18 months and are fully grown at two years.

Medical Research

Many common marmosets are used in research, since they are easy to handle and breed well in captivity. Because they are primates, much of their body chemistry is similar to that of humans, so scientists find it useful to study their biology and behavior. For those involved in biomedical research common marmosets provide a suitable model on which to test new drugs before they are tried on humans.

fluff up their fur, and show off their rumps and white genitals. If their warnings are not heeded, they will fight.

The common marmoset, like other marmosets and tamarins, lives on fruit and some small animal prey. It is particularly fond of juices (gums and sap) that seep from wounds in tree bark. The marmoset's lower front teeth are specially adapted for gouging holes in tree bark, from which the sweet, nutrient-rich sap oozes. Sap is especially important during the dry season when other food is in short supply. The animals will return repeatedly to trees that provide the valuable food.

Common name Emperor tamarin

Scientific name *Saguinus imperator*

Family	Callitrichidae
Order	Primates
Size	Length head/body: 9–10.4 in (23–26 cm); tail length: 14–17 in (36–42 cm)

Weight 11–14 oz (300–400 g)

Key features	Small, lightweight monkey; gray coat; long, white mustache; crown silvery, tail reddish-orange
Habits	Active during the day among tree branches; lives in family groups of up to 15 members
Breeding	One or 2, rarely 3 young born after a gestation period of 140–145 days. Weaned at 2–3 months; sexually mature at 16–20 months. May live at least 20 years in captivity, usually fewer in the wild
Voice	Birdlike calls
Diet	Fruit, insects, and tree sap
Habitat	Tropical rain forest
Distribution	Amazon Basin; extreme southeastern Peru, northern Bolivia, and northwestern Brazil
Status	Population: unknown; IUCN Vulnerable (subspecies *S.i. imperator*); CITES II. Becoming threatened, especially because of habitat loss

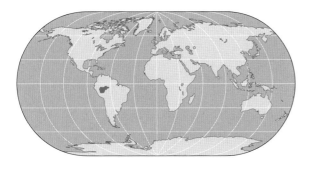

Emperor Tamarin

Saguinus imperator

Emperor tamarins have impressive long, white mustaches. As with other tamarins, they are social, living in small groups. They often share territory and feed with saddleback tamarins.

THE EMPEROR TAMARIN WAS SO named because of its long, white mustache, which resembled that of a famous 19th-century German emperor, Kaiser Wilhelm I. The mustache is so long that it reaches to the tamarin's shoulders when the two strands are laid back and is the animal's most distinctive and impressive feature. The body is mainly gray, with a mixture of fine yellow hair on the back and a rusty-red scattering of color on the chest. Emperor tamarins also have a silvery-brown crown, black hands and feet, and a reddish-brown tail. Like most tamarins, they have claws on all fingers and toes, except the big toe, which has a nail.

There are two subspecies. The bearded emperor tamarin (*S. imperator subgrisescens*) has a small white beard, which is lacking in the black-chinned emperor tamarin (*S. i. imperator*). Some scientists consider them to be two separate species.

Energetic Foragers

Emperor tamarins are lively animals, leaping and bounding through trees with quick, rather jerky movements. They spend the majority of their time foraging for food, using most levels of the forest. They venture to the ends of branches high in the trees to feed on ripe fruit and nectar, but tend to look for insects in the lower and middle levels of the forest canopy. They carefully inspect the leaves and branches, picking off insects as they find them. Stick insects, mantises, and other large insects make up most of their diet, together with ants, spiders, small animals such as lizards, and probably occasional birds' eggs. They also eat tree gum where it leaks from damaged bark. To get at it, they may leave the branches and cling to the side of the tree, embedding their claws into the bark to support their weight.

Emperor tamarins live in groups of up to 15 individuals, although between five and eight is more common. Within each group there are two or more unrelated adults, together with offspring of varying ages. Each group has a home range of between 25 and 100 acres (10 and 40 ha). The size of the range depends on the amount of food available, the size of the group, and whether the area is shared with another species of tamarin. The tamarins mark their home ranges using urine and scent from

The emperor tamarin can be recognized by its distinctive mustache. It feeds at all levels of the forest, but mainly in the upper layers. The smaller saddleback tamarin catches insects that drop to the lower levels as a result of the emperor's feeding technique.

glands around the base of the tail. Unlike the sprawling posture used by species of tamarin that have neck or chest glands, emperor tamarins smear the scent onto the branches while in a sitting position. They also notify other tamarins of their presence with birdlike calls. When necessary, they will chase away intruders.

Mixed Troops

Emperor tamarins often live with other tamarin species, particularly the saddleback tamarin. The two species will share a territory, each using the same boundaries. Saddleback tamarins are smaller and more agile than emperors, so they will often reach a food supply first. However, the larger emperors are dominant and will chase the saddlebacks away if there is not enough food to go around. Despite occasional conflicts over food supplies, both animals seem to benefit from the association, since it increases their chances of spotting predators. Emperors seem to be better at detecting aerial predators, such as hawks, while saddlebacks are better at spotting ground predators, such as snakes or small cats. The two species exchange calls and are able to coordinate their movements even if they cannot see each other in the dense forest.

Emperor tamarins mate in May and June, which means the young are born at the start of the rainy season in October to November. A male courts the breeding female by opening his mouth, waggling his tongue, and producing a high-pitched trill.

Newborn emperor tamarins weigh about 1.2 ounces (35 g) and have a coat of short hair. As with other tamarins, mothers feed the babies every few hours, then return them to the father or other group members for carrying. The young ride on an adult's back until they are about six or seven weeks old. After that they become increasingly independent. When they are able to take solid food, all the group members help feed them.

Lemurs

The lemurs are an extremely diverse group. They have been separated from other primates for millions of years, isolated on the island of Madagascar. Over time they have evolved into many different species with a wide variety of characteristics and behaviors. Being an island, Madagascar offers limited physical space to the species that live there. The animals are found in all the forested areas, with different species using different types of habitat. Some have been introduced to the nearby Comoro Islands.

Family Lemuridae (typical lemurs): 4 genera, 10 species

Lemur 1 species, ringtailed lemur (*L. catta*)

Eulemur 5 species, including black lemur (*E. macaco*); mongoose lemur (*E. mongoz*); crowned lemur (*E. coronatus*)

Varecia 1 species, ruffed lemur (*V. variegata*)

Hapalemur 3 species, bamboo lemur (*H. griseus*); golden bamboo lemur (*H. aureus*); greater bamboo lemur (*H. simus*)

Family Megaladapidae (sportive lemurs): 1 genus, 7 species

Lepilemur includes weasel sportive lemur (*L. mustelinus*); Milne-Edwards's sportive lemur (*L. edwardsi*)

Family Cheirogaleidae (dwarf and mouse lemurs): 5 genera, 13 species

Microcebus 8 species, including gray mouse lemur (*M. murinus*); pygmy mouse lemur (*M. myoxinus*); brown mouse lemur (*M. rufus*)

Mirza 1 species, Coquerel's dwarf lemur (*M. (microcebus) coquereli*)

Allocebus 1 species, hairy-eared dwarf lemur (*A. trichotis*)

Cheirogaleus 2 species, greater dwarf lemur (*C. major*); fat-tailed dwarf lemur (*C. medius*)

Phaner 1 species, fork-marked lemur (*P. furcifer*)

Family Indriidae (indris, sifakas, and woolly lemurs): 3 genera, 6 species

Avahi 2 species, eastern woolly lemur (*A. laniger*); western woolly lemur (*A. occidentalis*)

Propithecus 3 species, golden-crowned sifaka (*P. tattersalli*); diademed sifaka (*P. diadema*); Verreaux's sifaka (*P. verreauxi*)

Indri 1 species, indri (*I. indri*)

Family Daubentoniidae: 1 genus, 1 species

Daubentonia aye-aye (*D. madagascariensis*)

A Brief History of Lemurs

All lemurs have come from a single ancestor, perhaps just one pregnant female, which arrived on Madagascar about 40 million years ago. The animal probably drifted to the island on a raft of floating vegetation. Over thousands of years the offspring multiplied and adapted to different habitats and ways of life, until about 50 different species had evolved on the island. But then, about 2,000 years ago humans arrived. Within a few hundred years—a blink of an eye in terms of primate evolution—hunting and habitat destruction had wiped out many of the species. The largest were the giant sloth lemurs, known from skeletons found in caves. Today, of the 37 species of lemur several are threatened with extinction, and many are under pressure, especially from loss of habitat.

Lemurs exhibit a wide range of size, habits, diet, reproductive, and social behavior. They also live in habitats as diverse as evergreen rain forest and spiny, deciduous desert forests. Some lemurs are active in the daytime, while others only come out at night. They eat almost all things that other primates are known to eat, from insects to leaves and fruit. Their social behavior ranges from solitary animals that live and forage alone to large, mixed-sex groups. The smallest lemur (and smallest primate) is the pygmy mouse lemur, which weighs about 1 ounce (30 g), only slightly more than a house mouse. One of the giant sloth lemurs would have held the record for being the largest primate—at 440 pounds (200 kg) or so, bigger than a full-grown male gorilla.

1a   1b   2a   2b

⊝ *In one genus, Eulemur, the coat color is different in males and females. Here, male black lemur (1a); female black lemur (1b); male mongoose lemur (2a); female mongoose lemur (2b).*

⊖ *Milne-Edwards's lemurs, like other sportive lemurs, rest in hollow trees during the day as a way of conserving energy.*

(Inset): Energy-rich nectar forms an important part of the diet of all dwarf and mouse lemurs.

Common Features

Although they are a diverse group, lemurs have many features in common. They all have a long, foxlike face, apart from the bamboo lemurs. Their ears are at least partially hairy, and the naked areas of their hands and feet have ringed pads. All lemurs, except the indri, have a long, furry tail, but it is not strong enough to hang by alone. Lemurs seem to use their sense of smell more than other primates, and scent marking is a common way of labeling territory. Ringtailed lemurs sometimes have "smell fights." They cover their tail in scent from glands on the wrists, then wave it, wafting the smell at their opponents. Typical lemurs include the ringtailed lemur

(often kept in zoos) and brown lemurs. They are mostly cat-sized with a long tail. The coat color is variable, and some species have face stripes, patches, or beards. Typical lemurs are tree-living, except the ringtailed lemur, which prefers to travel on the ground. Most eat a range of plants and insects, but the bamboo lemurs are vegetarian, having specialized in bamboo shoots.

Sportive lemurs are medium-sized creatures weighing less than 2.2 pounds (1 kg). They are possibly the smallest mammals in the world that feed only on leaves. Leaves are not rich in energy, so sportive lemurs spend little time foraging and many hours resting and digesting food. They also have a lower metabolic rate than other animals of their size, so their body burns up fuel more slowly.

Dwarf and mouse lemurs are tiny. They have large eyes associated with a nocturnal lifestyle. Some use their tail for fat storage. Storing fat helps keep them going during the dry season when food is short—something that no other primate does.

Members of the Indriidae family are relatively large animals with long, powerful legs for leaping between trees. Indris spend most of their time high in the treetops, eating leaves, fruit, and flowers. Small groups of indris defend territories with scent marking and loud calls, including duets that sound like those of gibbons.

The aye-aye is the only living member in its family. It has a unique appearance, including long, thin middle fingers, which it uses to probe for insects in holes and crevices. Aye-ayes have peculiar teeth too, with two large front incisors, like those of rodents.

Common name Ringtailed lemur

Scientific name *Lemur catta*

Family   Lemuridae

Order   Primates

Size   Length head/body: 15–18 in (38–45 cm); tail length: 22–25 in (56–63 cm)

Weight   5–7.7 lb (2.3–3.5 kg)

Key features Cat-sized animal with dense, pale-gray fur; underparts pale; white face with black eye patches; long black-and-white banded tail, usually held upright

Habits   Active during the day; feeds in trees but also spends a lot of time on the ground

Breeding Single infant (occasionally twins) born between August and November after gestation period of approximately 136 days. Weaned at 4 months; sexually mature at 2 or 3 years. May live over 30 years in captivity, fewer in the wild

Voice   Catlike mews, grunts, yaps, howls, and purrs

Diet   Mainly fruit; also leaves, bark, and sap

Habitat   Dry deciduous scrub and forest

Distribution South and southwestern Madagascar

Status   Population: fewer than 100,000; IUCN Endangered; CITES II. Declining due to loss of habitat

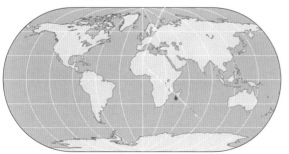

Ringtailed Lemur

Lemur catta

With their distinctive banded tail—useful as a flag and in "stink fights"—ringtailed lemurs are unmistakable animals. They breed well in captivity and are the most common lemur kept in zoos.

RINGTAILED LEMURS ARE SOCIABLE animals. They live in groups of between three and 25 animals, although about 14 is the average. The groups, called troops, contain animals of both sexes and all ages. There is a well-defined hierarchy dominated by the females. In each troop there is a top, or "alpha," female who is dominant over the group as a whole. The males have their own hierarchy. There is one central male who is more likely to interact with the females in the group than any of the others.

The troop spends a lot of time interacting socially. The lemurs seem to love close bodily contact, and often huddle together to snooze in a mass of fur and tails. Social grooming is important to reinforce bonds of friendship, especially among the females. When grooming, they use their hands and lower teeth. The lower incisors stick straight out from the lower jaw to form a "grooming comb."

Home Patch

Each troop has a home range, the size of which depends on the quality of the habitat. Important resources within the habitat include the number of fruiting trees and sources of water. Home ranges also change with the seasons and vary between 15 and 75 acres (6 and 30 ha), with the larger ranges being in open forest or dry brush and scrub. Each day the lemurs travel about half a mile (1 km) in search of food. Sometimes their home ranges overlap with those of other groups. Meetings are rare, but in confrontations it is the females that are responsible for defending the group.

that they use to rub the scent into the tender bark of young saplings.

Fruits of the Forest

Ringtailed lemurs feed at all levels in the forest, from the thin branches at the tops of trees to the forest floor. They use their hands to pull branches close, then bite off morsels of food to chew. They rarely use their hands to peel, pick, or prepare food. The ringtailed lemur has a varied diet, taking food from many different types of plants. Occasionally, it will also feed on insects and birds' eggs. The majority of its diet is fruit, with that of the introduced tamarind tree being a particular favorite. It also eats leaves, bark, and sap. Sometimes it raids crops, eating melons and the leaves of sweet potato plants.

Ringtails are active during the day, with two main periods of feeding separated by a rest period at midday. At night they sleep up in the trees. They spend more time on the ground than any other lemur (about one-third of their day) and tend to travel on the ground rather than through the branches of trees. In many typical areas of dry habitat trees are often widely spaced—a feature that probably dictates the lemurs' preference for ground travel; to make progress, they would have to keep coming down to the ground anyway. When walking on all fours, the hind end of a ringtailed lemur is held high because its arms are so short. The tail is lifted into a question-mark shape and used a bit like a flag to keep group members together. When traveling, the animals use clear routes through the forest, so they are often seen on roads and human paths.

Ringtailed lemurs are extremely vocal animals. They use about 15 different calls to maintain contact, indicate aggression, and warn each other of danger. Calls are especially important in dense forests when group

① *A ringtailed lemur drinks from a river on a private reserve in Madagascar. Ideal ringtail habitat—dry deciduous scrub and forests on the edges of rivers—is fast disappearing.*

Conflicts usually begin with a staring match between rival lemurs, followed by lunging approaches that only occasionally lead to physical aggression. After a confrontation the excited group will return to the safety of the core of their home range.

Ringtailed lemurs mark out their range with scent. Females use scent from their genitals and smear it onto branches. The males have scent glands just above their wrists, with a horny pad members may not be able to see each other. Many of their noises are catlike. They use a "meow" to keep the group together when traveling and are even known to purr when contented. Rapid staccato grunts signal aggression between two individuals. Males use a loud, penetrating howl that can be heard up to half a mile (1 km) away to announce their presence and possession of their home range. Ringtailed lemurs use different alarm calls to distinguish between aerial threats (such as flying hawks) and ground-based predators.

Expressive Gestures

Lemurs greet each other with a tap on the nose. Although they are not as expressive as some primates, various expressions are used in face-to-face communication. When threatening each other or mobbing a predator, they will stare fiercely, with their eyes wide and mouth open, but the teeth covered. The lips can be drawn back to reveal the teeth in a "scream face," used when retreating in terror. The teeth are also revealed in a more relaxed situation to communicate submission or a friendly approach. When making contact calls or

⊕ *A female ringtailed lemur with her young. Immediately after birth the infant clings to its mother's underside. At two weeks it begins to ride on her back.*

Sunbathing Spirits

The local name for the ringtailed lemur is "*Maki.*" Local people consider the animals to be the spirits of the dead returned to the world to worship the sun. Ringtailed lemurs love to sunbathe, especially early in the morning before feeding. They sit up with their bent legs splayed, exposing their bellies to the sun. Their arms are held high or resting on their knees. They look like furry sun worshippers meditating in a yoga position.

begging for food, ringtails open their eyes wide and push their lips into an "O" shape.

Ringtailed lemurs become sexually mature at two or three years old, and females will probably have a baby every year. Once they are mature, the males always leave the group in which they were born, and established males will change groups every three to five years. Ringtailed lemurs mate between mid-April and mid-May. The timing ensures that the young will be weaned in a period when food is abundant. When the females are fertile, their genitals swell and turn pink. A receptive female will turn a normally calm group of males into a frenzy of sexual excitement. They make loud, aggressive challenges to each other for the chance to mate. Males also hold "stink fights" in which they wipe the scent from their wrist glands onto their long, bushy tails, then waft the scent at the opposition. Presumably, the smelliest tail wins. Such contests are usually enough for the lemurs to decide who is dominant, but sometimes fights break out.

Most young are born in August and September, with a few late arrivals in November. There is usually one baby, although twins do occur occasionally. Immediately after birth the baby clings to the mother's underside, but after a couple of weeks it starts to ride on her back. All adult females help in raising the group's young. They baby-sit, form playgroups, and even switch babies so they are sometimes breast-feeding another's offspring. If an infant is orphaned, the group will adopt it. Other group members are allowed to groom the young. The infants seem to spend a lot of time having their faces licked, which they do not seem to enjoy!

At two and a half months a young lemur gains a little more independence and begins to play with other youngsters in the group. It spends the next few weeks exploring its environment, tasting plants, and climbing around in the trees. However, it will still ride on its mother's back when the group is traveling. Young are weaned at about four months old, but many do not survive. Around half die in their first year, and only about a third reach adulthood. Most are killed by predators. Birds of prey such as harrier hawks and buzzards will take babies, and both the adults and young are hunted by the fossa, a strange catlike creature that is unique to Madagascar.

Shrinking Habitats

Ringtailed lemurs breed remarkably well in captivity, and over 1,000 now live in about 140 zoos around the world. However, the species is disappearing rapidly in the wild. The main problem is that habitats in which ringtails can thrive are shrinking fast.

The most suitable habitats for ringtailed lemurs are gallery forests. They are narrow bands of forest that are found along the edges of rivers. Dry Euphorbia scrub also provides a good living for ringtailed lemurs. However, people are destroying such areas with fires, overgrazing, and through the harvesting of wood to make charcoal. Ringtailed lemurs are still hunted in some places, and a few are trapped and kept as pets.

⊕ *A troop of ringtailed lemurs gathers in a tree. The animals are highly companionable and enjoy close bodily contact. Sometimes they huddle together to snooze.*

Common name Aye-aye

Scientific name *Daubentonia madagascariensis*

Family Daubentoniidae

Order Primates

Size Length head/body: 12–15 in (30–38 cm); tail length: 17–22 in (43–56 cm)

Weight 4.4–6.6 lb (2–3 kg)

Key features Largest nocturnal lemur; long, shaggy coat, dark gray-brown; tail long and bushy; short face with round, pink nose, large ears, and large, orange eyes; hands with long, thin fingers and long, nail-like claws; middle finger elongated and bony

Habits Nocturnal; mainly solitary

Breeding Single baby born every 2–3 years after gestation period of 170 days. Weaned at 7 months; sexually mature at 2–3 years. May live about 23 years in captivity, over 20 in the wild

Voice Variety of calls, including a short "cree"

Diet Insect larvae and fruit, including coconuts and mangoes

Habitat Rain forest, humid forest, deciduous forest, mangroves, thickets, and plantations

Distribution Eastern and northern Madagascar, with small population on western side

Status Population: unknown, perhaps a few thousand; IUCN Endangered; CITES I. Like other lemurs, at risk when forest cut down. Feared as bad omen and killed on sight; some shot by farmers; a few killed to eat. Very rare

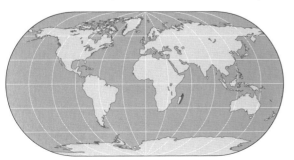

Aye-Aye

Daubentonia madagascariensis

The aye-aye is a bizarre creature that looks like nothing else on earth. It uses its long, bony middle finger to winkle out wood-boring grubs and to extract the flesh of coconuts.

THE AYE-AYE IS AN INCREDIBLY strange animal. With its shaggy coat, long bushy tail, enormous leathery ears, orange eyes, and bony hands it looks more like a Spielberg creation than a real animal. Its hands are the most unusual feature. Each finger is long and thin, but the third fingers are even longer than the others and very skinny. The aye-aye also has long front teeth (incisors) that keep growing throughout the animal's life. Continuously growing incisors are a major feature in all rodents, but not in any other primate. As a result, when first discovered, the aye-aye was classified as a squirrel-like rodent.

Specialized Diet

The aye-aye has a very unusual diet, specializing in insect grubs and the inside of nuts. Its mode of feeding is linked to its unusual body features. With its long front teeth it gnaws a hole in the hard outer cover of nuts such as coconuts. It then uses its long, thin middle finger to extract the fleshy interior. It eats insect grubs in a similar way. It finds them by tapping on wood and using its large ears to locate the sound of movement inside. Then it gnaws through the wood and pokes out the grub, again using its specially elongated middle finger.

Aye-ayes are mainly solitary. Nevertheless, small groups are sometimes seen outside the breeding period, particularly at sites where food is plentiful. They are nocturnal, spending their day alone in nests. The nests are built high in the trees and made of twigs and leaves. Each animal uses several nests within its range. Aye-ayes often sleep in each other's nests, so several different animals may occupy the same nest over a few weeks, just as we might use a motel.

Aye-ayes usually become active just before sunset. The males tend to appear first and start their evening with a bout of loud calls that ring through the forest. They spend most of the night foraging and can travel up to 2.5 miles (between 2 and 4 km). Females are less wide ranging. Bouts of foraging are interspersed with rest periods that may last a couple of hours. Aye-ayes walk and jump using all fours. They are agile, leaping and climbing between vertical tree trunks and branches with confidence. They move more deliberately on the ground, but can still travel fairly long distances between trees.

Each aye-aye has a home range that it marks with urine and scent. The home range of males is large, between 250 and 500 acres (100 and 200 ha). Such ranges often overlap with other males, and encounters between the animals can become aggressive. Female home ranges are much smaller, at 75 to 120 acres (30 to 50 ha). They do not generally overlap with each other, and females usually fight on the rare occasions when they meet.

Female aye-ayes can breed in any season. When receptive, they advertise their state with loud calls. Several males may be attracted to a female, and fights often break out. When she has mated, the female moves to another area and begins calling again. As a result, she may mate with several males.

Aye-Aye Surveys

Aye-ayes were once thought to be restricted to a few lowland rain forests along the east coast of Madagascar. However, after intensive surveys they have now been found over a wider area and in many more types of habitat. As well as dense forest, they also live in mangroves, thickets, and even plantations of fruit such as coconut and lychee. They are shy and difficult to see, but gnaw marks on nuts and fibrous fruits are signs of their presence.

⊕ *A six-month-old aye-aye. For the first two months the mother leaves the baby in a nursery nest, rather than carrying it with her while foraging. Young are not weaned until they are at least seven months old.*

Common name Ruffed lemur

Scientific name *Varecia variegata*

Family   Lemuridae

Order   Primates

Size   Length head/body: 20–22 in (51–56 cm); tail length: 22–26 in (56–66 cm)

      Weight 7.3–10 lb (3.3–4.5 kg)

      Key features Large lemur with long, dense fur, especially around neck; 2 subspecies: black-and-white ruffed lemur has patched black-and-white coat; red-ruffed lemur is chestnut-red with black legs, face, and tail; white patch on neck

Habits   Lives in flexible, mixed-sex groups; spends most of its time in trees; active during the day and the early part of the night, with peaks of activity in the morning and again in the late afternoon and early evening

Breeding   Two to 4 young born after gestation period of 90–102 days. Weaned at 4–5 months; sexually mature at 2–4 years. May live over 30 years in captivity, slightly fewer in the wild

Voice   Variety of calls, including loud barks and roars

Diet   Mainly fruit; also nectar, leaves, seeds, and occasional small birds and rodents

Habitat   Primary and secondary rain forest

Distribution Eastern Madagascar

Status   Population: fewer than 29,000; IUCN Critically Endangered (subspecies *V. v. ruber*), Endangered (subspecies *V. v. variegata*); CITES II. Declining due to habitat loss; vulnerable to removal of fruit trees

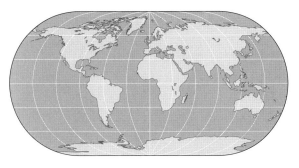

Ruffed Lemur   *Varecia variegata*

Ruffed lemurs are the largest members of the lemur family and have the most fruit-based diet. Unlike most primates, their litters contain many offspring.

RUFFED LEMURS ARE THE LARGEST of the true lemurs and have rich, dense fur, particularly around their neck and ears. There are two distinct-looking subspecies: the black-and-white ruffed lemur (*Varecia variegata variegata*) and the red-ruffed lemur (*Varecia variegata rubra*). The black-and-white ruffed lemur has furry ears, and its neck, back, sides, rump, and outside of the legs are white. It is black on the rest of the body. In complete contrast, the red-ruffed lemur is a rich chestnut-red color, with a dark face, hands, feet, and tail, and a creamy-white patch at the back of the neck. A few animals have white marks at their wrists and ankles, and some are also marked on the rump and muzzle.

Social Life

Ruffed lemurs are social animals and usually live in small, flexible groups of between five and 16 animals. Each group includes several adult males and females, plus their offspring. In some parts of their range, however, the lemurs appear to live as monogamous pairs. During the wet periods of the year many animals gather at fruiting trees, then disperse into smaller groups during the dry season. Each group has a home range of about 50 acres (20 ha), although occasionally groups may range over as much as 500 acres (200 ha). The animals focus their activities around the largest fruiting trees, where they feed and rest. The lemurs travel up to a mile (1.6 km) within their home range every day searching for food.

The group defends its territory against other groups of lemurs. The animals use loud barking calls to announce their presence, which are usually answered by neighboring lemurs. The calls, together with scent marking, provide warning signs and usually help avoid direct

confrontations. If two groups meet, they use intimidating barking in an aggressive standoff, which may end in a real fight.

Ruffed lemurs use many types of call. As well as territorial barks, they also have a variety of warning calls. The warnings sound different according to the type of threat involved, whether bird of prey, snake, or other mammal, for example. Ruffed lemurs also sound the "all clear" when the danger has passed and sometimes roar loudly to intimidate intruders.

Ruffed lemurs eat a great deal more fruit than the other lemurs, with the food forming approximately three-quarters of their diet. But they will also eat leaves, seeds, and even soil. Nectar is popular, but it is only available for a short time each year. However,

⊖ *The two distinct subspecies of ruffed lemur: black-and-white (inset) and red-ruffed (below). Coat patterns vary throughout the lemurs' range. Farther north the animals appear mainly black, while in the south they look whiter.*

when plants are in flower, their nectar is consumed in preference to any other food.

Nature's Helpers

A particularly important source of nectar is the travelers' palm. The lemurs use their strong hands to open the tough flower bracts, then poke their long muzzle deep inside the flowers to reach the nectar. In the process the lemurs get their face covered in pollen. When the animals move to other plants, they transfer the pollen between flowers. The ruffed lemur may be the only creature large and strong enough to pollinate this type of palm.

Ruffed lemurs mate between May and July. Most young are born the following September and October after a relatively short gestation. Twins and triplets are common, but litters of four or even six have been recorded. Instead of the usual two nipples of other primates, a ruffed lemur mother has six so that she can feed all her babies at once. Unlike most other lemurs, the mother leaves her babies in a nest. After one or two weeks she moves the babies, carrying them in her mouth as a cat carries kittens. When they are a little older, she "parks" them in a tree while she forages.

Young ruffed lemurs develop incredibly quickly. By three weeks they are able to move around among the trees, following their mother. They keep in contact with her using vocal calls. By four months the youngsters are as active and as agile as their parents.

Lower Primates

Lorises, pottos, bush babies, and tarsiers are small, nocturnal, tree-living primates. Although they share many features with early primates, they are not "primitive," since they have evolved many specialized characteristics. Recent research suggests that tarsiers are not closely related to lorises, pottos, and bush babies, despite having features in common. Certain tarsier characteristics, including features of their eyes, have encouraged some zoologists to group them with the higher primates (monkeys and apes).

Lorises, Pottos, and Bush Babies

Lorises, pottos, and bush babies are related to the lemurs, and together the groups form the lower primates or strepsirhines. Lorises and pottos are grouped together in

Family Galagonidae (bush babies): 4 genera, 17 species

Euoticus 2 species, southern needle-clawed galago (*E. elegantulus*); northern needle-clawed galago (*E. pallidus*)

Galago 6 species, including Gabon galago (*G. gabonensis*); Senegal galago (*G. senegalensis*); Somali galago (*G. gallarum*)

Galagoides 7 species, including Demidoff's bush baby (*G. demidoff*); Zanzibar galago (*G. zanzibaricus*); Thomas's galago (*G. thomasi*)

Otolemur 2 species, thick-tailed galago (*O. crassicaudatus*); Garnett's galago (*O. garnettii*)

Family Loridae (lorises and pottos): 5 genera, 7 species

Loris 1 species, slender loris (*L. tardigradus*)

Nycticebus 2 species, slow loris (*N. coucang*); pygmy loris (*N. pygmaeus*)

Arctocebus 2 species, golden potto (*A. aureus*); angwantibo (*A. calabarensis*)

Perodicticus 1 species, potto (*P. potto*)

Pseudopotto 1 species, Martin's false potto (*P. martini*)

Family Tarsiidae (tarsiers): 1 genus, 5 species

Tarsius includes western tarsier (*T. bancanus*); spectral tarsier (*T. spectrum*); pygmy tarsier (*T. pumilus*)

the family Loridae. Bush babies (sometimes called galagos) form another family called the Galagonidae.

Lorises, pottos, and bush babies have large eyes with a reflective layer at the back (the *tapetum lucidum*) to capture as much light as possible at night. They have little or no color vision. Their hands have fleshy pads at the fingertips, which give them a good grip, and thumbs that can reach around branches. However, the animals are incapable of delicate manipulation, since the thumb cannot touch each finger separately. The fingers and toes have nails, except the second toe, which has a claw and is modified for grooming. The forward-pointing front teeth are also modified for grooming the fine, fluffy fur. In addition, the animals use their teeth for gouging the bark of trees to feed on the sap that oozes out.

Lorises, pottos, and bush babies are mainly carnivorous, feeding on insects and a few small birds and reptiles. They tend to be solitary feeders, communicating with each other by calls and smells. They use excreta and scent from glands on their body to mark out their territory among the tree branches. Like lemurs, but unlike some other primates, they have a keen sense of smell.

All 17 species of bush baby live in Africa. The name bush baby is highly appropriate because they have large eyes, live in the bush, and sometimes wail like babies.

A thick-tailed galago. The loud croaking noise made by some bush babies is said to sound like the crying of a child.

The slender loris (1) has a mobile hip joint for climbing. A potto (2) hangs from a branch. An angwantibo from Africa (3). The rat-sized tarsier: here, spectral (4) and western species (5).

4

5

Bush babies are vocal animals. They use a variety of calls to maintain contact, attract mates, repel rivals, or sound the alarm. They are slender, with long legs for leaping. The tail is long and bushy and used for balancing. Bush babies have very large, mobile ears. When hunting, they usually hear their prey before they see it. They eat gum from damaged trees plus insects, particularly moths. Bush babies catch insects in flight by grabbing them with their hands.

Lorises live in Asia, and pottos are found in the rain forests of West Africa. Both animals are more ponderous than bush babies. They move hand over hand, foot over foot along the branches, taking extreme care with every step. They are equally comfortable walking on top of a branch or hanging below. Their limbs are roughly the same length, and they have flexible wrists and ankles. They can maintain a strong grip for hours at a time with the help of special blood vessels that supply oxygen to the tensed muscles of the hands and feet. The tail is stumpy, unlike the long, fluffy balancing aid of the bush babies. To match their slow lifestyle, lorises and pottos take mostly slow food, chiefly caterpillars and beetles.

Tarsiers

So far, five species of tarsier are known. But they are so small and difficult to study, especially in the dark, that there may be others as yet undiscovered. All live in the tropical rain forests of Southeast Asia—on the equatorial islands of Borneo, Indonesia, and the Philippines.

Tarsiers are roughly rat sized, except for the pygmy tarsier, which is smaller. They are entirely carnivorous, feeding on insects, birds, and snakes, and have been known to catch birds much larger than themselves. Their most distinctive feature is their eyes. They are huge and, relative to body size, the largest of any mammal. Each of the western tarsier's eyes weighs more than its brain. The large size may help compensate for the lack of a *tapetum lucidum*. Tarsiers also have a fovea, a spot at the back of the eye used for pin-sharp focusing. It is also found in higher primates, including humans.

Common name Slow loris

Scientific name
Nycticebus coucang

Family   Lorisiidae

Order   Primates

Size   Length head/body: 10–15 in (25–38 cm); tail length: 2 in (5 cm)

Weight 0.8–4.5 lb (0.3–2 kg)

Key features Plump animal with dense, woolly coat; red-gray to gray-brown with paler underside; dark stripe along back and dark circles around large eyes; pale muzzle and small ears; arms and legs same length, tail short

Habits   Very slow moving; lives in trees; generally solitary

Breeding   One, occasionally 2, young born any time of year after gestation period of 185–197 days. Weaned at 6 months; sexually mature at 18–24 months. May live up to 26 years in captivity, probably fewer in the wild

Voice   Whistles, growls, snarls, chirrs, and buzzing noises

Diet   Insects (often foul smelling or poisonous); mollusks (such as giant snails); lizards, small birds and mammals, and eggs; some plant food, including gum and fruit; finds most of its food by smell

Habitat   Tropical rain forest

Distribution Southeast Asia and western Indonesia

Status   Population: unknown, possibly about 1 million; CITES II. Not yet threatened, but declining due to habitat loss

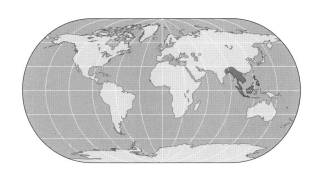

108   **SEE ALSO** Bush Baby, Demidoff's 4:110

Slow Loris

Nycticebus coucang

True to their name, slow lorises are not the fastest or brightest of primates. They rely on a tight grip for clinging to branches, stealth for hunting, and poison glands for defense.

LORISES ARE DIFFICULT TO SEE in the wild, since they are nocturnal and spend nearly all their time high in the canopy of rain forests. Dense bamboo thickets are another hiding place. Even when a loris is nearby, it is often difficult to spot because it keeps so still.

Slow lorises are rabbit-sized animals with short, dense, woolly fur. They are plumper and shorter limbed than their relatives the slender lorises. Their coat color is variable, ranging from a reddish-brown to pale brown-gray, and the fur often has a frosted look because of white tips to the hairs. They have a dark-brown stripe that runs along the back, forking at the head to behind the ears. The large eyes, typical of a nocturnal mammal, are ringed with dark fur. They have a paler stripe between them, which runs down the nose. Like other lorises, slow lorises have almost no tail.

Slowly but Surely

Slow lorises move slowly and deliberately, almost as in a slow-motion film. They travel carefully along branches, moving a hand first, then getting a secure grip before moving a foot. Their hands and feet are perfect for grasping, with the thumbs and big toes pointing sideways from the rest of the digits. An unusual arrangement of blood vessels helps the animals grip tightly for many hours without their muscles getting tired. Even when first born, slow lorises have a powerful, instinctive grip for clinging to their mother's fur.

During the day slow lorises sleep in holes and crevices, bamboo thickets, or in the fork of a tree. Gripping tightly with the hands and feet, they curl into a ball and tuck their head between their thighs.

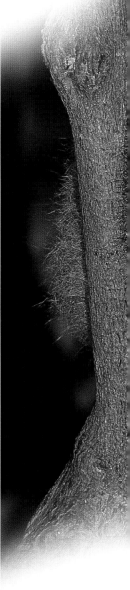

chest, arms, and palms. Smells help them recognize each other and detect who has been passing by.

Toxic Substance

Slow lorises are one of the few mammals that produce poison. They have glands on their arms that exude a smelly substance that is toxic when mixed with saliva. They spread the secretion from their arms all over their body when they groom, using their tooth-comb (specially modified front teeth). They also exude the poison when confronted by a predator, such as a snake. If the unpleasant smell does not warn off the attacker, the loris either uses the quickest means of escape—letting go of the branch and falling to the ground—or it will roll into a tight ball. A rolled-up loris is shielded from attack by tough humps on its back made by the backbones covered in thick skin. The poisonous secretions on its fur are distasteful and put many predators off eating lorises.

Slow lorises can breed at any time of year. When the female is receptive, males are attracted by the smell of her urine. When a male is in sight, she uses a rising and falling whistle to encourage him. Lorises mate hanging upside down.

A mother will often "park" her baby while she forages, even when it is only a couple of weeks old. Before leaving it—clinging tightly to a branch—she will cover it in saliva and probably also the smelly, poisonous secretion from her arm glands. The scent will protect the baby from predators. Infants become more active at six to eight weeks, but the mother will still carry her baby around until it is nearly as large as herself. The young become sexually mature at 18 to 24 months old. When the young males mature, their father will chase them out of his territory.

⊕ *Slow lorises come out at night to forage. Although generally slow moving, they can strike surprisingly fast when hunting. They creep up silently on their prey, then lunge at it, grabbing it with both hands.*

Slow lorises are believed to be solitary, although pairs may spend some time together. It is not unknown for males to occasionally help with rearing offspring. While foraging, slow lorises whistle loudly to each other. The call lets the animals know where the others are so that they can keep their distance.

Males have territories that overlap with those of several females, and such areas are diligently marked with urine. The lorises urinate on their hands and feet and wipe them on branches, leaving smelly footprints as they walk. Lorises also have scent glands on their face,

Common name
Demidoff's
bush
baby
(Demidoff's dwarf galago)

Scientific name *Galagoides demidoff*

Family Galagonidae

Order Primates

Size Length head/body: 3–6 in (7–15 cm); tail length: 8–10 in (20–26 cm)

Weight 1.5–3.4 oz (43–96 g)

Key features Gray-black to reddish coat with paler yellowish underparts; white stripe between eyes and down bridge of nose; pointed, upturned nose and relatively short ears

Habits Nocturnal; lively: runs along branches and leaps in tree canopy; sleeps in hollow trees, dense vegetation, or in nests; females may sleep in huddles of 10 or more; forages alone

Breeding Usually 1 young, sometimes 2, born per year after gestation period of 110–114 days. Weaned at 2 months; sexually mature at 8–9 months. May live 12 or more years in captivity, probably fewer in the wild

Voice Series of loud chirps, increasing to a crescendo; buzzing alarm call

Diet Insects: mainly beetles, moths, caterpillars, and crickets; also gum (tree sap) and some fruit

Habitat Dense secondary growth; forest edges or land running along the sides of roads

Distribution Equatorial western and central Africa

Status Population: relatively abundant; CITES II. Numerous in places, although not often seen

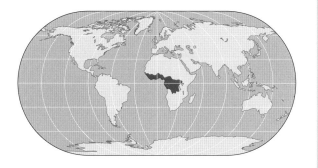

Demidoff's Bush Baby

Galagoides demidoff

Demidoff's bush baby is the smallest primate in Africa. It lives in dense vegetation in the understory of equatorial African forests.

DEMIDOFF'S BUSH BABY (otherwise known as Demidoff's galago) is one of four species of dwarf bush babies. Members of all four species look alike and are usually identified by their distinctive calls. However, scientists are still not sure how many species of bush baby there are, or how they are related to each other. They hope to resolve the mystery by studying the bush babies' calls and analyzing differences in their DNA (genetic molecular structure).

Tiny Balls of Fluff

Demidoff's bush babies are tiny, barely larger than a mouse. Like other bush babies, they are cute bundles of fur, with a large head and big eyes. They have a gray-black to reddish-brown body, with paler yellowish underparts. The color of the fur varies between individuals and according to age, younger animals being darker. The ears are relatively short for a bush baby, and the nose is pointed and upturned. There is a distinct white stripe running between the eyes and down the nose. The tail is long, but not as thick as in other bush babies.

Demidoff's bush babies live in dense vegetation. They prefer the lower levels of a forest, usually within 16 feet (5 m) of the ground. High-quality habitats attract large numbers of animals—as many as 260 per square mile (100 per sq. km).

In the center of forests the trees usually grow close together, and there is too little light for the type of shrubby growth that the bush baby needs. Consequently, the animals tend to be found on the edges of forests or along roadsides. They also favor patches where a fallen tree has allowed light to reach the forest

A Demidoff's bush baby in the rain forest of the Democratic Republic of Congo, formerly Zaire. Demidoff's bush babies are nocturnal, sleeping during the day in hollow trees or nests.

floor, conditions in which dense shrubs and young trees can proliferate. Bush babies are able to inhabit the small islands of forest that are left when trees are cut down. In fact, they may be one of the few mammals that actually benefit from tree felling and road building.

Demidoff's bush babies are lively and agile, running along narrow branches with ease. In dense, tangled vegetation they do not usually need to make the huge jumps that other bush babies are capable of, although horizontal leaps of 5 to 6.5 feet (1.5 to 2 m) have been known.

Like other bush babies, Demidoff's bush babies are nocturnal. They spend the day sleeping in hollow trees, thick vegetation, or in nests that they weave from leaves and twigs. The animals usually sleep alone, but sometimes groups of females and their young huddle together. They are active for most of the night, with just a brief rest at around midnight. They forage alone, but use contact calls so that they know where other animals are. Sound and scent are the main ways of communicating, and smell is also important in finding food after dark in the dense African forests.

Competing for Territory

Each male has a home range of about 2.5 acres (1 ha) that overlaps with the smaller ranges of several females. Competition for good areas containing many females may be intense, and adult males are aggressive toward each other when they meet. The bush babies mark their territories using scent glands and urine. By urinating on their hands and feet, they spread their personal scent wherever they walk.

Females usually give birth once a year to one or sometimes two babies. Demidoff's bush babies have the shortest gestation period of any bush baby—about 111 days. They can mate all year round, but births tend to peak at the time when food is most abundant.

Newborn young are tiny and weigh less than half an ounce (5 to 10 g). Although the mother is normally tolerant of other females, she does not allow another near her for the first couple of weeks after she has given birth. When the babies are a few days old, their mother carries them away from the nest and leaves them hidden in vegetation while she forages during the night. In the morning she carries them back. After about a month the young are able to follow the female, but she still carries them occasionally. If she jumps a gap that is too large for the young to cross alone, they call her back, and she carries them across.

Demidoff's bush babies eat mainly insects. Beetles, moths, caterpillars, and crickets are favorites. They have a higher proportion of insect protein in their diet (at about 70 percent) than larger species of bush babies. They also sometimes eat fruit. During the dry season they occasionally eat the gum (sticky sap) that oozes from trees where the bark has been damaged.

List of Species

The following lists all species of primates:

Order Primates
Primates

Suborder Strepsirhini
Lower primates (Strepsirhines)

FAMILY LEMURIDAE
Typical lemurs

Eulemur
E. coronatus Crowned lemur
E. fulvus Brown lemur
E. macaco Black lemur
E. mongoz Mongoose lemur
E. rubriventer Red-bellied lemur
Hapalemur
H. aureus Golden bamboo lemur
H. griseus Bamboo lemur
H. simus Greater bamboo lemur
Lemur
L. catta Ringtailed lemur
Varecia
V. variegata Ruffed lemur

FAMILY MEGALADAPIDAE
Sportive lemurs

Lepilemur
L. dorsalis Gray-backed sportive lemur
L. edwardsi Milne-Edwards' sportive lemur
L. leucopus White-footed sportive lemur
L. microdon Small-toothed sportive lemur (light-necked sportive lemur)
L. mustelinus Weasel sportive lemur
L. ruficaudatus Red-tailed sportive lemur
L. septentrionalis Northern sportive lemur

FAMILY CHEIROGALEIDAE
Dwarf and mouse lemurs

Allocebus
A. trichotis Hairy-eared dwarf lemur
Cheirogaleus
C. major Greater dwarf lemur
C. medius Fat-tailed dwarf lemur
Microcebus Mouse lemurs
M. berthae Berthe's mouse lemur
M. griseorufus Gray-brown mouse lemur
M. murinus Gray mouse lemur
M. myoxinus Pygmy mouse lemur
M. ravelobensis Golden-brown mouse lemur
M. rufus Brown mouse lemur
M. sambiranensis Sambirano mouse lemur
M. tavaratra Northern rufous mouse lemur
Mirza Dwarf lemurs
M. (Microcebus) coquereli Coquerel's dwarf lemur (mouse lemur)

Phaner
P. furcifer Fork-marked dwarf lemur

FAMILY INDRIIDAE
Indri, sifakas, and woolly lemurs

Avahi
A. laniger Eastern woolly lemur
A. occidentalis Western woolly lemur
Indri
I. indri Indri
Propithecus
P. diadema Diademed sifaka
P. tattersalli Golden-crowned sifaka
P. verreauxi Verreaux's sifaka

FAMILY DAUBENTONIIDAE
Aye-aye

Daubentonia
D. madagascariensis Aye-aye

FAMILY GALAGONIDAE
Bush babies and galagos

Euoticus
E. elegantulus Southern needle-clawed galago (elegant galago)
E. pallidus Northern needle-clawed galago (pale galago)
Galago
G. alleni Allen's galago
G. gabonensis Gabon galago
G. gallarum Somali galago
G. matschiei Eastern needle-clawed galago (Matschie's galago)
G. moholi Mohol galago (southern lesser galago)
G. senegalensis Senegal galago (lesser bush baby)
Galagoides
G. demidoff Demidoff's galago (dwarf bush baby or galago)
G. granti Grant's galago
G. orinus Mountain galago
G. rondoensis Rondo galago
G. thomasi Thomas's galago
G. udzungwensis Matundu galago
G. zanzibaricus Zanzibar galago
Otolemur
O. crassicaudatus Thick-tailed galago
O. garnettii Garnett's galago

FAMILY LORIDAE
Lorises and pottos

Arctocebus
A. aureus Golden potto
A. calabarensis Angwantibo
Loris
L. tardigradus Slender loris
Nycticebus
N. coucang Slow loris
N. pygmaeus Pygmy loris
Perodicticus
P. potto Potto
Pseudopotto
P. martini Martin's false potto

FAMILY TARSIIDAE
Tarsiers

Tarsius
T. bancanus Western tarsier
T. dianae Dian's tarsier
T. pumilus Pygmy tarsier
T. spectrum Spectral or eastern tarsier
T. syrichta Philippine tarsier

Suborder Haplorhini
Higher primates (tarsiers, monkeys, and apes)

FAMILY CALLITRICHIDAE
Marmosets and tamarins

Callimico
C. goeldii Goeldi's monkey
Callithrix Marmosets
C. aurita Buffy-tufted-ear marmoset
C. flaviceps Buffy-headed marmoset
C. geoffroyi Geoffroy's marmoset
C. jacchus Common marmoset
C. kuhlii Wied's black-tufted-ear marmoset
C. penicillata Black-tufted-ear marmoset
Cebuella
C. (Callithrix) pygmaea Pygmy marmoset
Leontopithecus Lion tamarins
L. caissara Black-faced lion tamarin
L. chrysomelas Golden-headed lion tamarin
L. chrysopygus Black lion tamarin
L. rosalia Golden lion tamarin
Mico
M. (Callithrix) argentata Silver marmoset
M. (Callithrix) chrysoleucus Golden-white tassel-ear marmoset
M. (Callithrix) emiliae Snethlage's marmoset
M. (Callithrix) humeralifer Santarém marmoset
M. (Callithrix) humilis Dwarf marmoset
M. (Callithrix) intermedius Aripuanã marmoset
M. (Callithrix) leucippe Golden-white bare-ear marmoset
M. (Callithrix) marcai Marca's marmoset
M. (Callithrix) mauesi Maués marmoset
M. (Callithrix) melanurus Black-tailed marmoset
M. (Callithrix) nigriceps Black-headed marmoset
Saguinus Tamarins
S. bicolor Pied tamarin
S. graellsi Graell's black-mantle tamarin
S. fuscicollis Saddleback tamarin
S. geoffroyi Geoffroy's tamarin
S. imperator Emperor tamarin
S. inustus Mottle-faced tamarin
S. labiatus Red-bellied tamarin

S. leucopus Silvery-brown tamarin (white-footed tamarin)
S. martinsi Bare-face tamarin
S. midas Red-handed tamarin
S. mystax Mustached tamarin
S. niger Black-handed tamarin
S. nigricollis Black-mantle tamarin
S. oedipus Cotton-top tamarin
S. tripartitus Golden-mantle saddleback tamarin

FAMILY CEBIDAE
Capuchinlike monkeys

Alouatta Howler monkeys
A. belzebul Red-handed howler
A. caraya Black-and-gold howler
A. fusca Brown howler
A. palliata Mantled howler
A. pigra Mexican black howler (Guatemalan howler)
A. seniculus Red howler
Aotus Night monkeys
A. nigriceps Southern night monkey (red-necked night monkey, owl monkey, douroucouli)
A. trivirgatus Northern night monkey (gray-necked night monkey, owl monkey, douroucouli)
Ateles Spider monkeys
A. belzebuth Long-haired spider monkey (white-bellied spider monkey)
A. chamek Black-faced black spider monkey
A. fusciceps Brown-headed spider monkey
A. geoffroyi Black-handed spider monkey
A. marginatus White-whiskered spider monkey
A. paniscus Black spider monkey
Brachyteles
B. arachnoides Muriqui (woolly spider monkey)
Cacajao Uakaris
C. calvus Red uakari (white uakari)
C. melanocephalus Black uakari (black-headed uakari)
Callicebus Titi monkeys
C. cupreus (superspecies group contains: *C. dubius, C. caligatus, C. olallae, C. modestus, C. oenanthe,* chestnut-bellied titi)
C. moloch (superspecies group contains: *C. cinerascens, C. hoffmannsi, C. brunneus, C. donacophilus,* dusky titi)
C. personatus Masked titi
C. torquatus Yellow-handed titi (white-handed titi, widow monkey, collared titi)
Cebus Capuchin monkeys
C. albifrons White-fronted capuchin
C. apella Brown capuchin (tufted or black-capped capuchin)

C. capucinus White-faced capuchin (white-throated capuchin)

C. olivaceus Weeper capuchin (wedge-capped capuchin)

Chiropotes Bearded sakis

C. albinasus White-nosed saki

C. satanas Bearded saki (black saki)

Lagothrix Woolly monkeys

L. flavicauda Yellow-tailed woolly monkey

L. lagotricha Humboldt's woolly monkey (smoky or common woolly monkey)

Pithecia Saki monkeys

P. aequatorialis Equatorial saki

P. albicans Buffy saki

P. irrorata Bald-faced saki

P. monachus Monk saki (red-bearded saki)

P. pithecia Guianan saki (white-faced saki)

Saimiri Squirrel monkeys

S. boliviensis Bolivian squirrel monkey

S. oerstedii Red-backed squirrel monkey

S. sciureus Common squirrel monkey

S. ustus Golden-backed squirrel monkey

FAMILY CERCOPITHECIDAE
Old World monkeys

SUBFAMILY CERCOPITHECINAE
Baboons, drills, mandrills, guenons, and macaques

Allenopithecus

A. nigroviridis Allen's swamp monkey

Cercocebus Mangabeys

C. galeritus Agile mangabey (crested or Tana River managbey)

C. torquatus White mangabey (collared, red-capped, or sooty mangabey)

Cercopithecus Guenons

C. albogularis Sykes' monkey

C. ascanius Redtail monkey (coppertail monkey, Schmidt's guenon)

C. campbelli Campbell's monkey

C. cephus Mustached monkey

C. diana Diana monkey

C. dryas Dryas monkey (salongo monkey)

C. erythrogaster Red-bellied monkey

C. erythrotis Red-eared monkey (Sclater's monkey)

C. hamlyni Owl-faced monkey (Hamlyn's monkey)

C. lhoesti L'Hoest's monkey

C. mitis Blue monkey (silver, golden, or Samango monkey)

C. mona Mona monkey

C. petaurista Lesser spot-nosed monkey (lesser white-nosed monkey)

C. neglectus De Brazza's monkey

C. nictitans Spot-nosed monkey

(greater white-nosed monkey, hocheur)

C. pogonias Crowned guenon

C. solatus Suntailed monkey

C. wolfi Wolf's monkey

Chlorocebus

C. aethiops Vervet (grivet, savanna, or green monkey)

Erythrocebus

E. patas Patas monkey (military or hussar monkey)

Lophocebus

L. albigena Gray-cheeked mangabey

L. aterrimus Black mangabey

Macaca Macaques

M. arctoides Stump-tailed macaque (bear macaque)

M. assamensis Assamese macaque

M. cyclopis Formosan rock macaque (Taiwan macaque)

M. fascicularis Long-tailed macaque (crab-eating or cynomolgous macaque)

M. fuscata Japanese macaque

M. maura Moor macaque

M. mulatta Rhesus macaque (rhesus monkey)

M. nemestrina Pig-tailed macaque

M. nigra Black macaque

M. pagensis

M. radiata Bonnet macaque

M. silenus Lion-tailed macaque

M. sinica Toque macaque

M. sylvanus Barbary macaque (Barbary ape or rock ape)

M. thibetana Tibetan macaque (Père David's or Tibetan stump-tailed macaque)

M. tonkeana Tonkean macaque

Mandrillus

M. leucophaeus Drill

M. sphinx Mandrill

Miopithecus

M. talapoin Talapoin monkey

Papio hamadryas

P. h. cynocephalus Yellow baboon

P. h. anubis Olive baboon

P. h. ursinus Chacma baboon

P. h. papio Guinea baboon

P. h. hamadryas Hamadryas baboon (sacred baboon)

Savanna baboon (common baboon)

Theropithecus

T. gelada Gelada (gelada baboon)

SUBFAMILY COLOBINAE
Colobus and leaf monkeys

Colobus

C. angolensis White-epauletted black colobus (Angolan black or black-and-white colobus)

C. guereza Guereza (white-mantled or magistrate black colobus, eastern black-and-white colobus)

C. polykomos Gray-epauletted black colobus (king or western black-and-white colobus)

C. satanas Satanic black colobus

C. vellerosus White-thighed black colobus (ursine black-and-white colobus)

Nasalis

N. (Simias) concolor Simakobu (pig-tailed snub-nosed monkey, Pagai Island langur)

N. larvatus Proboscis monkey

Presbytis Surelis

P. comata Grizzled sureli (gray or Sunda Island sureli)

P. femoralis Banded sureli

P. fredericae Fuscous sureli

P. frontata White-fronted sureli

P. melalophos Mitered sureli (black-crested sureli or simpai)

P. potenziani Mentawai sureli (red-bellied sureli)

P. rubicunda Red sureli (maroon sureli)

P. siamensis Pale-thighed sureli

Procolobus Red colobus monkeys

P. badius Western red colobus (bay colobus)

P. kirkii Dark-handed red colobus (Kirk's red colobus)

P. pennantii Pennant's red colobus

P. preussi Preuss' red colobus

P. tholloni Red-crowned red colobus (Thollon's or tshuapa red colobus)

P. verus Olive colobus (Van Beneden's colobus)

Pygathrix

P. (Rhinopithecus) avunculus Tonkin snub-nosed monkey (Dollman's snub-nosed monkey)

P. (Rhinopithecus) bieti Yunnan snub-nosed monkey (black snub-nosed monkey)

P. (Rhinopithecus) brelichi Guizhou snub-nosed monkey (gray or oxtailed snub-nosed monkey)

P. nemaeus Red-shanked douc monkey (cochin China monkey)

P. nigripes Black-shanked monkey (black-footed douc monkey)

P. (Rhinopithecus) roxellana Golden snub-nosed monkey (orange, snub-nosed, or Roxellane's monkey, moupin langur)

Semnopithecus Langurs and leaf monkeys

S. entellus Hanuman langur (common or gray langur)

S. hypoleucos Malabar langur

Trachypithecus semnopithecus

T. s. auratus Spangled leaf monkey (ebony or moor, or negro leaf monkey)

T. s. barbei Barbe's leaf monkey

T. s. cristatus Silvered leaf monkey

T. s. delacouri White-rumped black leaf monkey

T. s. geei Golden leaf monkey

T. s. hatinhenis Bar-headed black leaf monkey (ha tinh black leaf monkey)

T. s. francoisi White-sideburned black leaf monkey (Francois' black leaf monkey)

T. s. johnii Hooded black leaf monkey (leonine or gray-headed black leaf monkey or Nilgiri langur)

T. s. laotum White-browed black leaf monkey

T. s. mauritius Ebony leaf monkey (Moor or Negro leaf monkey)

T. s. obscurus Dusky leaf monkey (spectacled leaf monkey)

T. s. pileatus Capped leaf monkey (bonneted leaf monkey)

T. s. vetulus Purple-faced leaf monkey (wanderoo)

FAMILY HYLOBATIDAE
Gibbons

Hylobates

H. agilis Agile gibbon

H. concolor Crested black gibbon (concolor or white-cheeked gibbon)

H. gabriellae Yellow-cheeked crested gibbon (buff-cheeked gibbon)

H. hoolock Hoolock gibbon (white-browed gibbon)

H. klossi Kloss gibbon (Mentawai gibbon, beeloh; incorrectly: dwarf gibbon, dwarf siamang)

H. lar Lar gibbon (white-handed or common gibbon)

H. leucogenys Northern and southern white-cheeked crested gibbons

H. moloch Moloch gibbon (silvery gibbon)

H. muelleri Müller's gibbon (gray gibbon)

H. pileatus Pileated gibbon (capped gibbon)

H. syndactylus Samang

FAMILY HOMINIDAE
Great apes

Gorilla Gorillas

G. beringei Eastern gorilla

G. gorilla Western gorilla

Homo

H. sapiens Human

Pan Chimpanzees

P. paniscus Bonobo (dwarf or pygmy chimpanzee)

P. troglodytes Common chimpanzee

Pongo Orangutans

P. abelii Sumatran orangutan

P. pygmaeus Bornean orangutan

Glossary

Words in SMALL CAPITALS refer to other entries in the glossary.

Adaptation features of animal that adjust it to its environment; may be produced by evolution—e.g., camouflage, coloration

Adaptive radiation when a group of closely related animals (e.g., members of a FAMILY) have evolved differences from each other so that they can survive in different NICHES

Adult a fully grown animal that has reached breeding age

Anal gland (anal sac) a gland opening by short duct either just inside anus or on either side of it

Aquatic living in water

Arboreal living up among the branches of trees

Arthropod animals with a jointed outer skeleton e.g., crabs and insects

Biodiversity a variety of SPECIES and the variation within them

Biomass the total weight of living material

Biped any animal that walks on two legs. See QUADRUPED

Breeding season the entire cycle of reproductive activity from courtship, pair formation (and often establishment of TERRITORY), through nesting to independence of young

Browsing feeding on leaves of trees and shrubs

Bushmeat general name given (especially in West Africa) to meat from wild animals, often collected and sold illegally

Cache hidden supply of food; also (verb) to hide food for future use

Callosities hardened, thickened areas on the skin (e.g., ischial callosities in some PRIMATES)

Canine (tooth) a sharp stabbing tooth usually longer than rest

Canopy continuous (closed) or broken (open) layer in forests produced by the intermingling of branches of trees

Capillaries tiny blood vessels that convey blood through organs from arteries to veins

Carnassial (teeth) opposing pair of teeth especially adapted to shear with a cutting (scissorlike) edge; in living mammals the arrangement is unique to Carnivora, and the teeth involved are the fourth upper PREMOLAR and first lower MOLAR

Carnivore meat-eating animal

Carrion dead animal matter used as a food source by scavengers

Cecum a blind sac in the digestive tract, opening out from the junction between the small and large intestines. In herbivorous mammals it is often very large; it is the site of bacterial action on CELLULOSE. The end of the cecum is the appendix; in SPECIES with a reduced cecum the appendix may retain an antibacterial function

Cellulose the material that forms the cell walls of plants

Cementum hard material that coats the roots of mammalian teeth. In some SPECIES cementum is laid down in annual layers that, under a microscope, can be counted to estimate the age of individuals

Cheek pouch a pouch used for the temporary storage of food, found only in the typical monkeys of the OLD WORLD

Cheek teeth teeth lying behind the CANINES in mammals, consisting of PREMOLARS and MOLARS

Chromosomes strings of genetic material (DNA) within the cell nucleus; responsible for transmitting features from one generation to the next and for controlling cell growth and function

CITES Convention on International Trade in Endangered Species. An agreement between nations that restricts international trade to permitted levels through licensing and administrative controls. Rare animals and plants are assigned to categories: (for instance Appendix 1, 2). See Volume 1 page 17

Cloaca cavity in the pelvic region into which the gut, reproductive, and urinary ducts open. The cloaca forms a single opening to the body instead of a separate anus and openings for sexual and excretory activities

Congenital condition an animal is born with

Coniferous forest evergreen forests found in northern regions and mountainous areas dominated by pines, spruces, and cedars

Corm underground food storage bulb of certain plants

Crepuscular active in twilight

Cursorial adapted for running

Deciduous forest dominated by trees that lose their leaves in winter (or the dry season)

Deforestation the process of cutting down and removing trees for timber or to create open space for activities such as growing crops and grazing animals

Delayed implantation when the development of a fertilized egg is suspended for a variable period before it implants into the wall of the UTERUS and completes normal pregnancy. Births are thus delayed until a favorable time of year

Den a shelter, natural or constructed, used for sleeping, giving birth, and raising young; act (verb) of retiring to a den to give birth and raise young or for winter shelter

Dental formula a convention for summarizing the dental arrangement, in which the numbers of all types of tooth in each half of the upper and lower jaw are given. The numbers are always presented in the order: INCISOR (I), CANINE (C), PREMOLAR (P), MOLAR (M). The final figure is the total number of teeth to be found in the skull. A typical example for Carnivora is I3/3, C1/1, P4/4, M3/3 = 44

Dentition animal's set of teeth

Desert area of low rainfall dominated by specially adapted plants such as cacti

Diastema a space between the teeth, usually the INCISORS and CHEEK TEETH. It is typical of rodents and lagomorphs, although also found in UNGULATES

Digit a finger or toe

Digitigrade method of walking on toes without heel touching the ground. See PLANTIGRADE

Dispersal the scattering of young animals going to live away from where they were born and brought up

Display any relatively conspicuous pattern of behavior that conveys specific information to others, usually to members of the same SPECIES; can involve visual or vocal elements, as in threat, courtship, or greeting displays

Diurnal active during the day

DNA (deoxyribonucleic acid) the substance that makes up the main part of the CHROMOSOMES of all living things; contains genetic code that is handed down from generation to generation

Domestication process of taming and breeding animals to provide help and useful products for humans

Dormancy a state in which—as a result of hormone action—growth is suspended and metabolic activity reduced to a minimum

Dorsal relating to the back or spinal part of the body; usually the upper surface

Droppings see FECES and SCATS

Ecosystem a whole system in which plants, animals, and their environment interact

Echolocation the process of perception based on reaction to the pattern of reflected sound waves (echos); occurs in bats

Edentate toothless, but is also used as group name for anteaters, sloths, and armadillos

Endemic found only in one geographical area, nowhere else

Estivation inactivity or greatly decreased activity in hot or dry weather

Estrus the period when eggs are released from the female's ovaries, and she becomes available for successful mating. Estrous females are often referred to as "in heat" or as "RECEPTIVE" to males

Eutherian mammals that give birth to babies, not eggs, and rear them without using a pouch on the mother's belly

Euphorbia large cactuslike plants characteristic of SAVANNA regions of Africa

Excrement FECES

Extinction process of dying out in which every last individual dies, and SPECIES is lost forever

Family technical term for a group of closely related SPECIES that often also look quite similar. Zoological family names always end in "idae." See Volume 1 page 11. Also used as the word for a social group within a species made up of parents and their offspring

Feces remains of digested food expelled from the body as pellets. Often accompanied by SCENT secretions

Feral domestic animals that have gone wild and live independently of people

Flystrike where CARRION-feeding flies have laid their eggs on an animal

Fossorial adapted for digging and living in burrows or underground tunnels

Frugivore an animal that eats fruit as main part of the diet

Fur mass of hairs forming a continuous coat characteristic of mammals

Fused joined together

Gape wide-open mouth

Gene the basic unit of heredity enabling one generation to pass on characteristics to its offspring

Generalist an animal that is capable of a wide range of activities, not specialized

Genus a group of closely related SPECIES. The plural is genera. See Volume 1 page 11

Gestation the period of pregnancy in mammals, between fertilization of the egg and birth of the baby

Grazing feeding on grass

Gregarious living together in loose groups or herds

Harem a group of females living in the same TERRITORY and consorting with a single male

Herbivore an animal that eats plants (grazers and browsers are therefore herbivores)

Heterodont DENTITION specialized into CANINES, INCISORS, and PREMOLARS, each type of tooth having a different function. See HOMODONT

Homeothermy maintenance of a high and constant body temperature by means of internal processes; also called "warm-blooded"

Home range the area that an animal uses in the course of its normal periods of activity. See TERRITORY

Homodont DENTITION in which the teeth are all similar in appearance and function

Hybrid offspring of two closely related SPECIES that can interbreed, but the hybrid is sterile and cannot produce offspring of its own

Inbreeding breeding among closely related animals (e.g., cousins) leading to weakened genetic composition and reduced survival rates

Incisor (teeth) simple pointed teeth at the front of the jaws used for nipping and snipping

Indigenous living naturally in a region; NATIVE (i.e., not an introduced species)

Insectivore animals that feed on insects and similar small prey. Also used as a group name for animals such as hedgehogs, shrews, and moles

Interbreeding breeding between animals of different SPECIES or varieties within a single FAMILY or strain; interbreeding can cause dilution of the gene pool

Interspecific between SPECIES

Intraspecific between individuals of the same SPECIES

Invertebrates animals that have no backbone (or other true bones) inside their body, e.g., mollusks, insects, jellyfish, and crabs

IUCN International Union for the Conservation of Nature, responsible for assigning animals and plants to internationally agreed categories of rarity. See table below

Juvenile a young animal that has not reached breeding age

Kelp brown seaweeds

Keratin tough, fibrous material that forms hairs, feathers, and protective plates on the skin of VERTEBRATE animals

Lactation process of producing milk in MAMMARY GLANDS for offspring

Larynx voice box where sounds are created

Latrine place where FECES are left regularly, often with SCENT added

Mammary glands characteristic of mammals, glands for production of milk

Mangroves woody shrubs and trees adapted to living along muddy coasts in the tropics

Marine living in the sea

Matriarch senior female member of a social group

Metabolic rate rate at which chemical activities occur within animals, including the exchange of gasses in respiration and the liberation of energy from food

Metabolism the chemical activities within animals that turn food into energy

Migration movement from one place to another and back again, usually seasonal

Molars large crushing teeth at the back of the mouth

Molt process in which mammals shed hair, usually seasonal

Monogamous animals that have only one mate at a time

Monotreme egg-laying mammal, such as the duck-billed platypus

Montane in a mountain environment

Mutation random changes in genetic material

Native belonging to that area or country, not introduced by human assistance

IUCN CATEGORIES

EX Extinct, when there is no reasonable doubt that the last individual of a species has died.

EW Extinct in the Wild, when a species is known only to survive in captivity or as a naturalized population well outside the past range.

CR Critically Endangered, when a species is facing an extremely high risk of extinction in the wild in the immediate future.

EN Endangered, when a species faces a very high risk of extinction in the wild in the near future.

VU Vulnerable, when a species faces a high risk of extinction in the wild in the medium-term future.

LR Lower Risk, when a species has been evaluated and does not satisfy the criteria for CR, EN, or VU.

DD Data Deficient, when there is not enough information about a species to assess the risk of extinction.

NE Not Evaluated, species that have not been assessed by the IUCN criteria.

Natural selection when animals and plants are challenged by natural processes (e.g. predation, bad weather) to ensure survival of the fittest

New World the Americas; OLD WORLD refers to the non-American continents (not usually Australia)

Niche part of a habitat occupied by an ORGANISM, defined in terms of all aspects of its lifestyle

Nocturnal active at night

Nomadic animals that have no fixed home, but wander continuously

Old World non-American continents. See NEW WORLD

Olfaction sense of smell

Omnivore an animal that eats almost anything

Opportunistic taking advantage of every varied opportunity that arises; flexible behavior

Opposable fingers or toes that can be brought to bear against others on the same hand or foot in order to grip objects

Order a subdivision of a class of animals consisting of a series of related animal FAMILIES. See Volume 1 page 11

Organism any member of the animal or plant kingdom; a body that has life

Ovulation release of egg from the female's ovary prior to its fertilization

Pair bond behavior that keeps a male and a female together beyond the time it takes to mate; marriage is a "pair bond"

Parasite animal or plant that lives on or in body of another

Parturition process of giving birth

Pelage furry coat of a mammal

Pelagic living in upper waters of the open sea or large lakes

Pheromone SCENT produced by animals to enable others to find and recognize them

Physiology processes within plants and animal bodies, e.g., digestion. Maintaining a warm-blooded state is a part of mammal physiology

Placenta the structure that links an embryo to its mother during pregnancy, allowing exchange of chemicals between them

Plantigrade walking on soles of feet with heels touching the ground. See DIGITIGRADE

Polygamous when animals have more than one mate in a single mating season.

Polygynous when a male mates with several females in one BREEDING SEASON

Population a distinct group of animals of the same SPECIES or all the animals of that species

Posterior the hind end or behind another structure

Predator an animal that kills live prey for food

Prehensile grasping tail or fingers

Premolars teeth found in front of MOLARS, but behind CANINES

Pride social group of lions

Primate a group of mammals that includes monkeys, apes, and ourselves

Promiscuous mating often with many mates, not just one

Protein chemicals made up of amino acids. Essential in the diet of animals

Quadruped an animal that walks on all fours (a BIPED walks on two legs)

Range total geographical area over which a SPECIES is distributed

Receptive when a female is ready to mate (in ESTRUS)

Reproduction the process of breeding, creating new offspring for the next generation

Retina light-sensitive layer at the back of the eye

Riparian living beside rivers and lakes

Roadkill animals killed by traffic

Roost place that a bat or a bird regularly uses for sleeping

Rumen complex stomach found in RUMINANTS specifically for digesting plant material

Ruminant animals that eat vegetation and later bring it back from stomach to chew again ("chewing the cud" or

"rumination") to assist digestion by microbes in the stomach

Salivary glands glands in the mouth and throat that produce large amounts of watery secretion to aid chewing and digestion of food

Savanna tropical grasslands with scattered trees and low rainfall, usually in warm areas

Scats fecal pellets, especially of CARNIVORES. SCENT is often deposited with the pellets as territorial markers

Scent chemicals produced by animals to leave smell messages for others to find and interpret

Scrotum bag of skin in which the male testicles are located

Scrub vegetation dominated by shrubs—woody plants usually with more than one stem

Secondary forest trees that have been planted or grown up on cleared ground.

Siblings brothers and sisters

Social behavior interactions between individuals within the same SPECIES, e.g., courtship

Species a group of animals that look similar and can breed to produce fertile offspring

Steppe open grassland in parts of the world where the climate is too harsh for trees to grow

Sub-Saharan all parts of Africa lying south of the Sahara Desert

Subspecies a locally distinct group of animals that differ slightly from normal appearance of SPECIES; often called a race

Symbiosis when two or more SPECIES live together for their mutual benefit more successfully than either could live on its own

Syndactylous fingers or toes that are joined along their length into a single structure

Taxonomy branch of biology concerned with classifying ORGANISMS into groups according to similarities in their structure, origins, or behavior. The categories, in order of increasing broadness, are: SPECIES, GENUS, FAMILY, ORDER, class, and phylum. See Volume 1 page 11

Terrestrial living on land

Territory defended space

Thermoregulation the maintenance of a relatively constant body temperature either by adjustments to METABOLISM or by moving between sunshine and shade

Torpor deep sleep accompanied by lowered body temperature and reduced METABOLIC RATE

Toxins poisonous chemicals often produced by plants as a defense against being eaten by animals

Translocation transferring members of a SPECIES from one location to another

Tundra open grassy or shrub-covered lands of the far north

Underfur fine hairs forming a dense, woolly mass close to the skin and underneath the outer coat of stiff hairs in mammals

Ungulate hoofed animals such as pigs, deer, cattle, and horses; mostly HERBIVORES

Uterus womb in which embryos of mammals develop

Ultrasounds sounds that are too high-pitched for humans to hear

Ungulates hoofed animals

Ventral belly or underneath of an animal (opposite of DORSAL)

Vertebrate animal with a backbone (e.g., fish, mammals, reptiles), usually with skeleton made of bones, but sometimes softer cartilage

Vibrissae sensory whiskers, usually on snout, but can be on areas such as elbows, tail, or eyebrows

Viviparous animals that give birth to active young rather than laying eggs

Vocalization making of sounds such as barking and croaking

Yeti mysterious apelike creature reportedly inhabiting parts of Himalayas

Zoologist person who studies animals

Zoology the study of animals

Further Reading

General

Cranbrook, G., **The Mammals of Southeast Asia**, Oxford University Press, New York, NY, 1991

Eisenberg, J. F., and Redford K. H., **The Mammals of the Neotropics**, University of Chicago Press, Chicago, IL., 1999

Estes, R. D., **The Behavioral Guide to African Mammals**, University of California Press, Berkley, CA, 1991

Garbutt, N., **The Mammals of Madagascar**, Pica Press, Sussex, U.K., 1999

Kingdon, J., **The Kingdon Field Guide to African Mammals**, Academic Press, San Diego, CA, 1997

MacDonald, D., **Collins Field Guide to the Mammals of Britain and Europe**, Harper Collins, New York, NY., 1993

MacDonald, D., **The Encyclopedia of Mammals**, Barnes and Noble, New York, NY, 2001

Nowak, R. M., **Walker's Mammals of the World**, The John Hopkins University Press, Baltimore, MD, 1999

Skinner, J. D., and Smithers, R. H. N., **The Mammals of the Southern African Subregion**, University of Pretoria, Pretoria, South Africa, 1990

Wilson, D. E., and Reeder, D. M., **Mammal Species of the World. A Taxonomic and Geographic Reference**, Smithsonian Institute Press, Washington, DC, 1999

Young, J. Z., **The Life of Mammals: Their Anatomy and Physiology**, Oxford University Press, Oxford, U.K., 1975

Specific to this volume

Fossey, D., **Gorillas in the Mist**, Houghton Mifflin, New York, NY, 2000

Harcourt, C., and Thornback, J., **Lemurs of Madagascar**, IUCN, Switzerland and Cambridge, U.K., 1990

Heltne, P. G., and Marquardt, L. A., **Understanding Chimpanzees**, Harvard University Press, Cambridge, MA., 1989

Kaplan, G., and Rogers, L. J., **The Orangutans: Their Evolution, Behavior, and Future**, Perseus Group, New York, NY, 2000

Leakey, R., **The Making of Mankind**, Michael Joseph, London, U.K., 1981

Linden, E., **Apes, Men, and Language**, Dutton and Co., New York, NY., 1975

Nowak, R. M., **Walker's Primates of the World**, John Hopkins University Press, Baltimore, MD., 2000

Rowe, N., **The Pictorial Guide to the Living Primates**, Pogonias Press, East Hampton, NY., 1996

Russon, A. E., **Orangutans: Wizards of the Rain Forest**, Robert Hale, London, U.K., 1999

Sapolsky, R. M., **A Primate's Memoir: Love, Death, and Baboons in East Africa**, Jonathan Cape, London, U.K., 2001

Strum, S., **Almost Human: A journey into the World of Baboons**, Chicago University Press, Chicago, IL, 2002

Weber, B., and Vedder, A., **In the Kingdom of Gorillas**, Aurum Press, London, U.K., 2001

Useful Websites

General

http://animaldiversity.ummz.umich.edu/
University of Michigan Museum of Zoology animal diversity websites. Search for pictures and information about animals by class, family, and common name. Includes glossary

http://www.cites.org/
IUCN and CITES listings. Search for animals by scientific name, order, family, genus, species, or common name. Location by country and explanation of reasons for listings

http://endangered.fws.gov
Information about threatened animals and plants from the U.S. Fish and Wildlife Service, the organization in charge of 94 million acres (38 million ha) of American wildlife refuges

http://www.iucn.org
Details of species and their status; listings by the International Union for the Conservation of Nature, also lists IUCN publications

http://www.panda.org
World Wide Fund for Nature (WWF), newsroom, press releases, government reports, campaigns

http://www.aza.org
American Zoo and Aquarium Association

http://www.wcs.org
Website of the Wildlife Conservation Society

http://www.nwf.org
Website of the National Wildlife Federation

http://www.nmnh.si.edu/msw/
Mammals list on Smithsonian Museum site

http://www.press.jhu.edu/books/walkers_mammals_of_the_world/prep.html
Text of basic book listing species, illustrating almost every genus

Specific to this volume

http://www.primates_online.com
General website for information on primates

http://www.primate.org
General information and links on primates

Set Index

A **bold** number shows the volume and is followed by the relevant page numbers (e.g., **1:** 52, 74).

Common names in **bold** (e.g., **aardwolf**) mean that the animal has an illustrated main entry in the set. Underlined page numbers (e.g., **9:** 78–79) refer to the main entry for that animal.

Italic page numbers (e.g., **2:** *103*) point to illustrations of animals in parts of the set other than the main entry.

Page numbers in parentheses—e.g., **1:** (24)—locate information in At-a-Glance boxes.

Animals that get main entries in the set are indexed under their common names, alternative common names, and scientific names.

Picture Credits

Abbreviations

FLPA	Frank Lane Picture Agency
NHPA	Natural History Photographic Agency
NPL	naturepl.com
OSF	Oxford Scientific Films

t = top; b = bottom; c = center; l = left; r = right

Jacket

tl caracal, Pete Oxford/naturepl.com; tr group of dolphins, Robert Harding Picture Library; bl lowland gorilla, Martin Rügner/Naturphotographie; br Rothchild's giraffe, Gerard Lacz/FLPA

8–9 Staffan Widstrand/NPL; **10–11** Richard du Toit/NPL; **11** Steve Robinson/NHPA; **14–15**, **16–17**, **18** Anup Shah/NPL; **18–19** Tom Vezo/NPL; **20–21** Martin Harvey/NHPA; **22** Adrian Warren/Ardea; **23** Yann Arthus-Bertrand/Corbis; **24–25** C. & R. Aveling/ICCE; **26–27** Gerard Lacz/FLPA; **28–29** Ferrero-Labat/Ardea; **30**t Fritz Polking/FLPA; **30**b Miles Barton/NPL; **31** Clive Bromhall/OSF; **32–33** Anup Shah/NPL; **34–35** Chris Martin Bahr/Ardea; **37** M. Watson/Ardea; **38–39**, **41** Anup Shah/NPL; **42–43** James Carmichael Jr./NHPA;

44–45 Daniel J. Cox/OSF; **46–47** Jeff Foott/NPL; **47** Richard du Toit/NPL; **48–49**, **50–51** Jean-Paul Ferrero/Ardea; **52–53** Minden Pictures/FLPA; **54–55** Geoff Trinder/Ardea; **56** Adrian Warren/Ardea; **56–57** W. Wisniewski/FLPA; **57** T. Whittaker/FLPA; **58–59** P. & J. Wegner/Foto Natura/FLPA; **60–61** Zig Leszczynski/Animals Animals/OSF; **62–63** Konrad Wothe/OSF; **64–65** Alan Towse/Ecoscene; **66** J. Moore/Anthro-Photo; **67** Anup Shah/NPL; **68–69** Jurgen & Christine Sohns/FLPA; **70–71** Gerard Lacz/FLPA; **73** Roine Magnusson/Bruce Coleman Collection; **74–75**, **76–77** Kevin Schafer/NHPA; **78–79** Pete Oxford/NPL; **80–81** Nick Gordon/Ardea; **82–83** Joe B. Blossom/Survival Anglia/OSF; **84–85** Partridge Films Ltd/OSF; **87** M. Watson/Ardea; **88–89** E.A. Janes/NHPA; **90–91** Mike Lane/NHPA; **91** John Downer/NPL; **92–93**, **94–95** Gerard Lacz/FLPA; **97**l Pete Oxford; **97**r David Haring/OSF; **98–99**, **100**, **100–101** Pete Oxford/NPL; **102–103** David Haring/OSF; **104–105** Alan & Sandy Carey/OSF; **105** Kevin Schafer/NHPA; **107** Anthony Bannister/NHPA; **108–109** Martin Harvey/NHPA; **110–111** Bruce Davidson/NPL

Artists

Denys Ovenden, Priscilla Barrett with Michael Long, Graham Allen, Malcolm McGregor

While every effort has been made to trace the copyright holders of illustrations reproduced in this book, the publishers will be pleased to rectify any omissions or inaccuracies.